NURSING 3SS3

TABLE OF CONTENTS
& ACKNOWLEDGEMENTS

PAGE

BACKGROUND

Summary of Recommendations

This Guideline replaces the RNAO BPG *Assessment and Management of Stage I to IV Pressure Ulcers* (2007).

We have used these symbols for the recommendations:

✓　　No change was made to the recommendation as a result of the systematic review evidence.

+　　The recommendation and supporting evidence were updated with systematic review evidence.

NEW　A new recommendation was developed based on evidence from the systematic review.

PRACTICE RECOMMENDATIONS		LEVEL OF EVIDENCE	STATUS
1.0 Assessment	Recommendation 1.1: Conduct a health history, a psychosocial history, and a physical exam on initial examination and whenever there is a significant change in the person's medical status.	V	+
	Recommendation 1.2: Assess the risk for developing *additional* pressure injuries on initial examination and if there is a significant change in the person's medical status using a valid and reliable pressure injury risk assessment tool.	V	+
	Recommendation 1.3: Assess the person's pressure injury using the same valid and reliable wound assessment tool on initial examination and whenever there is a significant change in the pressure injury.	V	+
	Recommendation 1.4: Assess the person's pressure injury for signs and symptoms of infection (superficial critical colonization/localized infection and/or deep and surrounding infection/systemic infection) using a standardized approach on initial examination and at every dressing change.	V	NEW

	Recommendation 1.5: a) Screen all persons with pressure injuries for risk of malnutrition using a valid and reliable screening tool on first examination and if there is a delay in pressure injury healing. b) Determine the nutritional status of all persons at risk for malnutrition using a valid and reliable assessment tool within 72 hours of initial examination, and whenever there is a change in health status and/or the pressure injury. c) Perform a comprehensive nutrition assessment of all persons with poor nutritional status within 72 hours of initial examination, and if there is a change in health status or delayed healing.	V	**NEW**
	Recommendation 1.6: Assess for pressure injury pain on initial examination and continue to monitor pain at subsequent visits, including prior to and after every wound care intervention, using the same valid and reliable tool consistent with the person's cognitive ability.	V	**+**
	Recommendation 1.7: Perform a vascular assessment (i.e., medical history, physical exam) of all persons with pressure injuries in the lower extremities on initial examination.	V	**+**
	Recommendation 1.8: Conduct a mobility and support surface assessment on initial examination and whenever there is a significant change in the person's medical condition, weight, equipment, mobility, and/or pressure injury healing.	V	**+**
2.0 Planning	Recommendation 2.1: Obtain the referral or consultations required to plan and coordinate a pressure injury plan of care.	V	**+**
	Recommendation 2.2: Develop a pressure injury plan of care that incorporates goals mutually agreed upon by the person, the person's circle of care, and the interprofessional team.	Ia	**+**

2

BACKGROUND

PRACTICE RECOMMENDATIONS		LEVEL OF EVIDENCE	STATUS
3.0 Implementation	**Recommendation 3.1:** Reposition the person at regular intervals (i.e., every two to four hours) based on person-centred concerns. While sitting, weight-shift the person every 15 minutes.	V	+
	Recommendation 3.2: Position all persons with a pressure injury on a pressure redistribution support surface at all times.	V	+
	Recommendation 3.3: Implement an individualized nutritional plan of care in collaboration with the person and his/her circle of care that addresses nutritional requirements and provides adequate protein, calories, fluid, and appropriate vitamin and mineral supplementation to promote pressure injury healing.	V	+
	Recommendation 3.4: Provide local pressure injury care consisting of the following, as appropriate: ■ cleansing (level of evidence = V); ■ moisture balance (healable) or moisture reduction (non-healable, maintenance) (level of evidence = Ia–b, V); ■ infection control (i.e., superficial critical colonization/localized infection and/or deep and surrounding infection/systemic infection) (level of evidence Ia-b, V); and ■ debridement (level of evidence = V).	Ia, Ib, V	+
	Recommendation 3.5: Provide electrical stimulation (when available) as an adjunct to best practice wound care in order to speed healing and promote wound closure in stalled but healable stage 2, 3, and 4 pressure injuries.	Ia	+

	Recommendation 3.6: Implement, as an alternative, the following treatments in order to speed closure of stalled but healable pressure injuries, as appropriate and if available: ■ electromagnetic therapy (level of evidence = Ib), ■ ultrasound (level of evidence = Ib), and ■ ultraviolet light (level of evidence = Ib). Do not consider the following treatment in order to speed closure of stalled but healable pressure injuries: ■ laser therapy (not recommended) **STOP PRACTICE**	Ib	+
	Recommendation 3.7: Provide negative pressure wound therapy to people with stage 3 and 4 pressure injuries in exceptional circumstances, including enhancement of quality of life and in accordance with other person-/family-centred preferences.	V	+
	Recommendation 3.8: Collaborate with the person and his/her circle of care to implement a pressure injury self-management plan.	Ia	+
	Recommendation 3.9: Implement a person-centred pain management plan using pharmacological and non-pharmacological interventions.	V	+
4.0 Evaluation	**Recommendation 4.1:** Use the initial risk assessment tool to reassess the person's risk for developing additional pressure injuries on a regular basis and whenever a change in the person's health status occurs.	V	**NEW**
	Recommendation 4.2: Use the initial wound assessment tool to monitor the person's pressure injuries for progress toward person-centred goals on a regular basis and at dressing changes.	V	+

BACKGROUND

4

BACKGROUND

EDUCATION RECOMMENDATIONS		LEVEL OF EVIDENCE	STATUS
5.0 Education	Recommendation 5.1: Develop and implement comprehensive and sustainable interprofessional pressure injury education programs for clinicians and students entering health-care professions.	V	+
	Recommendation 5.2: Assess health-care professionals' knowledge, attitudes, and skills related to the assessment and management of existing pressure injuries before and following educational interventions using an appropriate, reliable, and validated assessment tool.	IV, V	+

SYSTEM, ORGANIZATION, AND POLICY RECOMMENDATIONS		LEVEL OF EVIDENCE	STATUS
6.0 System, Organization, and Policy	Recommendation 6.1: Organizations must lead and provide the resources to integrate pressure injury management best practices into standard and interprofessional clinical practice, with continuous evaluation of outcomes.	IV	+
	Recommendation 6.2: Lobby and advocate for investment in pressure injury management as a strategic quality and safety priority in jurisdictions in order to improve health outcomes for people with pressure injuries.	V	NEW

Appendix H: Pressure Injury Risk Assessment Tools

The most commonly used and validated risk assessment tools for adults are (in no particular order of importance):

- **the Braden Scale for Predicting Pressure Sore Risk** (Bergstrom, Braden, Kemp, Champagne & Ruby, 1988; Braden and Bergstrom, 1994; Garcia-Fernandez, Pancorbo-Hidalgo, & Agreda, 2014; Kring, 2007);

- **the Norton Scale** (Garcia-Fernandez et al., 2014);

- **the Waterlow Score** (Garcia-Fernandez et al., 2014); and

- **the Pressure Ulcer Risk Scale (PURS)** (Carreau, Niezgoda, Trainor, Parent, & Woodbury, 2015; Poss et al., 2010).

Studies have demonstrated that the above tools are reliable and valid (AWMA, 2012; NPUAP, EPUAP, & PPPIA, 2014; Perry et al., 2014; RNAO, 2011). They are currently endorsed by reputable guideline groups, such as the Australia Wound Management Association (AWMA), the Institute for Clinical Systems Improvement (ICSI), the National Pressure Ulcer Advisory Panel (NPUAP)/European Pressure Ulcer Advisory Panel (EPUAP), and Pan Pacific Pressure Injury Alliance (PPPIA).

The following is not an exhaustive list of pressure injury risk assessment tools. The tools below have been suggested as examples identified within the systematic review, AGREE II appraised guidelines, by the expert panel or external stakeholder feedback.

TOOL	VALIDATION STUDIES	WEBSITE ACCESS
Braden Scale	Bergstrom, N., Braden, B., Kemp, M., Champagne, M., & Ruby, E. (1998). Predicting pressure ulcer risk: A multi-site study of the predictive validity of the Braden scale. *Nursing Research, 47*(5), 261–9. Kring, D.L. (2007). Reliability and validity of the Braden Scale for Predicting Pressure Ulcer Risk. *Journal of Wound, Ostomy and Continence Nursing, 34*(4), 399–406. Garcia-Fernandez, E. P., Pancorbo-Hidalgo, P. L., & Agreda, J. J. (2014). Predictive capacity of risk assessment scales and clinical judgement for pressure ulcers: A meta-analysis. *Journal of Wound, Ostomy and Continence Nursing, 41*(1), 24–34.	http://www.education. woundcarestrategies.com/coloplast/ resources/BradenScale.pdf
Norton Scale	Garcia-Fernandez, E. P., Pancorbo-Hidalgo, P. L., & Agreda, J. J. (2014). Predictive capacity of risk assessment scales and clinical judgement for pressure ulcers: A meta-analysis. *Journal of Wound, Ostomy and Continence Nursing, 41*(1), 24–34.	http://www.health.vic.gov.au/__data/ assets/file/0010/233668/Norton-scale. pdf
Waterloo Pressure Ulcer Risk Assessment	Garcia-Fernandez, E. P., Pancorbo-Hidalgo, P. L., & Agreda, J. J. (2014). Predictive capacity of risk assessment scales and clinical judgement for pressure ulcers: A meta-analysis. *Journal of Wound, Ostomy and Continence Nursing, 41*(1), 24–34.	http://www.judy-waterlow.co.uk/ index.htm

TOOL	VALIDATION STUDIES	WEBSITE ACCESS
Pressure Ulcer Risk Scale (PURS)	Carreau, L., Niezgoda, H., Trainor, A., Parent, M., & Woodbury, M.G. (2015). Pilot study compares scores of the Resident Assessment Instrument Minimum Data Set version 2.0 (MDS 2.0) Pressure Ulcer Risk Scale with the Braden Pressure Ulcer Risk Assessment for Patients in Complex Continuing Care. *Advances in Skin and Wound Care, 28*(1), 28–33. Poss, J., Murphy, K. M., Woodbury, M. G., Orsted, H., Stevenson, K., Williams, G., ... Hirdes, J. P. (2010). Development of the interRAI Pressure Ulcer Risk Scale (PURS) for use in long-term care and home care settings. *BMC Geriatrics, 10*(67). doi:10.1186/1471-2318-10-67	http://ltctoolkit.rnao.ca/sites/ltc/files/resources/pressure_ulcer/AssessmentTools/AppedixkPUBPG.pdf Please refer to Appendix K: http://rnao.ca/sites/rnao-ca/files/storage/related/7749_PRESSURE-ULCERS_Supplement_2011.pdf

Appendix J: Progression from Bacterial Balance to Bacterial Damage

Contaminated or colonized	Bacteria are present on the wound surface (contaminated). A steady state of replicating organisms are attaching to the wound tissue and multiplying but they are not associated with tissue damage or delayed healing (colonization).	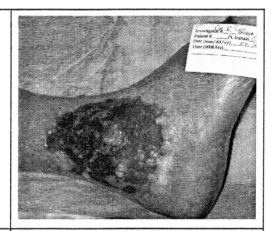
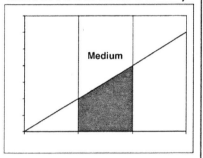		
Critically colonized (local infection, covert infection, increased bacterial burden)	• The bacterial burden in the wound bed is increasing. • Initiates the body's immune response (inflammation). • The wound is no longer healing at the expected rate: wound size is not decreasing. • Look for the signs outlined in the enabler NERDS.	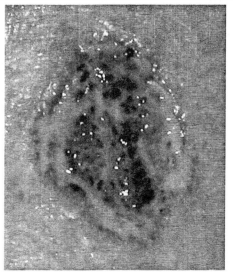
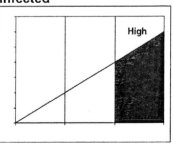		
Infected	• Bacteria are present within the wound and have spread to the deeper and surrounding tissue. They are multiplying and causing tissue damage. • There is an associated host inflammatory response that has now spread to the deeper tissue and surrounding skin. • The wound is painful and may increase in size with potential satellite areas of breakdown. • Look for the signs outlined in the enabler STONES.	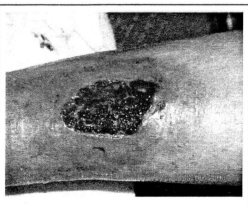

Summary *of* Recommendations

		RECOMMENDATION	*LEVEL OF EVIDENCE
Practice Recommendations	1	Nurses endorse the Baby-Friendly™ Hospital Initiative (BFHI), which was jointly launched in 1992 by the World Health Organization (WHO) and the United Nations Children's Fund (UNICEF). The BFHI directs health care facilities to meet the "Ten Steps to Successful Breastfeeding".	III
	1.1	Nurses have a role in advocating for "breastfeeding friendly" environments by: ※ advocating for supportive facilities and systems such as day-care facilities, "mother and baby" areas for breastfeeding, public breastfeeding areas, 24-hour help for families having difficulties in breastfeeding; and ※ promoting community action in breastfeeding.	III
	2	Nurses and health care practice settings endorse the WHO recommendation for exclusive breastfeeding for the first six months, with introduction of complementary foods and continued breastfeeding up to two years and beyond thereafter.	I
	3	Nurses will perform a comprehensive breastfeeding assessment of mother/baby/family, both prenatally and postnatally, to facilitate intervention and the development of a breastfeeding plan.	III
	3.1	Key components of the prenatal assessment should include: ※ personal and demographic variables that may influence breastfeeding rates; ※ intent to breastfeed; ※ access to support for breastfeeding, including significant others and peers; ※ attitude about breastfeeding among health care providers, significant others and peers; and ※ physical factors, including breasts and nipples, that may effect a woman's ability to breastfeed.	III

*See page 14 for details regarding "Interpretation of the Evidence"

RNAO

	RECOMMENDATION	LEVEL OF EVIDENCE
Practice Recommendations (cont.)	3.2 Key components of the postnatal assessment should include: ※ intrapartum medications; ※ level of maternal physical discomfort; ※ observation of positioning, latching and sucking; ※ signs of milk transfer; ※ parental ability to identify infant feeding cues; ※ mother-infant interaction and maternal response to feeding cues; ※ maternal perception of infant satisfaction/satiety cues; ※ woman's ability to identify significant others who are available and supportive of the decision to breastfeed; ※ delivery experience; and ※ infant physical assessment.	III
	3.3 Practice settings are encouraged to develop, adopt or adapt assessment tools encompassing key components for assessment and that meet the needs of their local practice setting.	III
	4 Nurses will provide education to couples during the childbearing age, expectant mothers/couples/families and assist them in making informed decisions regarding breastfeeding. Education should include, as a minimum, the following: ※ benefits of breastfeeding (Level I); ※ lifestyle issues (Level III); ※ milk production (Level III); ※ breastfeeding positions (Level III); ※ latching/milk transfer (Level II-2); ※ prevention and management of problems (Level III); ※ medical interventions (Level III); ※ when to seek help (Level III); and ※ where to get additional information and resources (Level III).	
	5 Small, informal group health education classes, delivered in the antenatal period, have a better impact on breastfeeding initiation rates than breastfeeding literature alone or combined with formal, non-interactive methods of teaching.	I

11

RNAO

RECOMMENDATION		LEVEL OF EVIDENCE
Practice Recommendations (cont.)	5.1 Evaluation of education programs should be considered in order to evaluate the effectiveness of prenatal breastfeeding classes.	II-2
	6 Nurses will perform a comprehensive breastfeeding assessment of mother/baby prior to hospital discharge.	III
	6.1 If mother and baby are discharged within 48 hours of birth, there must be a face-to-face follow up assessment conducted within 48 hours of discharge by a qualified health care professional, such as a Public Health Nurse or Community Nurse specializing in maternal/newborn care.	III
	6.2 Discharge of mother and baby after 48 hours should be followed by a telephone call within 48 hours of discharge.	III
	7 Nurses with experience and expertise in breastfeeding should provide support to mothers. Such support should be established in the antenatal period, continued into the postpartum period and should involve face-to-face contact.	I
	7.1 Organizations should consider establishing and supporting peer support programs, alone or in combination with one-to-one education from health professionals, in the antenatal and postnatal periods.	I
Education Recommendations	8 Nurses providing breastfeeding support should receive mandatory education in breastfeeding in order to develop the knowledge, skill and attitudes to implement breastfeeding policy and to support breastfeeding mothers.	II-2
Organization & Policy Recommendations	9 Practice settings need to review their breastfeeding education programs for the public and, where appropriate, make the necessary changes based on recommendations in this best practice guideline.	III
	10 Practice settings/organizations should work towards being accredited by the Baby-Friendly™ Hospital Initiative.	III

12

RNAO

Appendix E :
Postpartum Assessment Tools

Postpartum Assessment Tool	Reference
Infant Breastfeeding Assessment Tool (IBFAT)	See next page. Matthews, M.K. (1988). Developing an instrument to assess infant breastfeeding behaviour in the early neonatal period. *Midwifery, 4*(4), 154-165.
LATCH – Breastfeeding Charting System©	Jensen, D., Wallace, S., & Kelsay, P. (1994). LATCH: A breastfeeding charting system and documentation tool. *Journal of Obstetric, Gynecologic and Neonatal Nursing, 23*(1), 27-32.
Mother-Baby Assessment (MBA) Form	Mulford, C. (1992). The mother-baby assessment (MBA): An "Apgar Score" for breastfeeding. *Journal of Human Lactation, 8*(2), 79-82.

86

Infant Breastfeeding Assessment Tool (IBFAT)

Reprinted from: Matthews, M.K. (1988). Developing an instrument to assess infant breastfeeding behaviour in the early neonatal period. *Midwifery*, *4*(4), 154-165, with permission of Elsevier.

Infant Breastfeeding Assessment Tool (IBFAT)

Check the score which best describes the baby's feeding behaviours at this feed.

	3	2	1	0
In order to get baby to feed:	Placed the baby on the breast as no effort was needed.	Used mild stimulation such as unbundling, patting or burping.	Unbundled baby, sat baby back and forward, rubbed baby's body or limbs vigorously at beginning and during feeding.	Could not be aroused.
Rooting	Rooted effectively at once.	Needed coaxing, prompting or encouragement.	Rooted poorly even with coaxing.	Did not root.
How long from placing baby on breast to latch & suck?	0 – 3 minutes.	3 – 10 minutes.	Over 10 minutes.	Did not feed.
Sucking pattern	Sucked well throughout on one or both breasts.	Sucked on & off but needed encouragement.	Sucked poorly, weak sucking; sucking efforts for short periods.	Did not suck.

MOTHER'S EVALUATION
How do you feel about the way the baby fed at this feeding?
3 – Very pleased   2 – Pleased   1 – Fairly pleased   0 – Not pleased

IBFAT assigns a score, 0,1,2, or 3 to five factors. Scores range from 0 to 12.
The mother's evaluation score is not calculated in the IBFAT score.

Appendix F: Breastfeeding Positions

Cradle-Hold

This is a common position for breastfeeding. In order to latch the baby, the mother may support her breast with the hand opposite the side that the baby is nursing, with her thumb and fingers well back from the areola. Using the arm on the same side the baby is nursing on, the mother supports the baby's head and body and keeps the infant close. The baby should be at the level of the breast, and pillows are useful to provide additional support. The mother turns the baby towards her so that the infant's nose, chin, tummy and knees are touching her. The mother can tuck the infant's lower arm below her breast to keep it out of the way.

Modified Cradle-Hold

The mother should be seated comfortably with additional pillows as necessary to support her back and arms then tuck the baby under breast. Use of a footstool may be beneficial. The mother can support her breast with fingers positioned at the base of her breast well back from the areola. The baby should be held in the arm opposite to the breast being used. The baby's shoulder and neck are supported by her hand and the baby is turned facing the mother. Holding the back of the infant's head with her hand may cause the infant to pull away when being put onto the breast. The baby's head and neck should be in a slightly extended position to facilitate the chin touching the breast (Biancuzzo, 1999; Lothian, 1995).

Illustrations reproduced with the permission of the City of Ottawa.

88

Side-Lying

The mother should lie on her side with one or two pillows supporting her head and her lower arm flexed up. Use pillows as necessary to support her back and legs. The baby should be positioned side-lying, facing the mother, with the head low enough that the mom's nipple is at the level of the baby's nose, and the neck extended so that eye contact with the mother is possible (Scarborough Breastfeeding Network, 1999; Society of Paediatric Nursing of the Royal College of Nursing, 1998). **The mother's hand should be across baby's shoulder blades. The mother should pull the baby towards her abdomen, and wait. The baby will extend his head with a wide mouth and will latch onto the breast without assistance.**

Football Hold (Clutch Hold)

The mother should be seated comfortably as per the 'cradle-hold' description. The baby should be positioned on a pillow at the mother's side, on the side of the breast to be used. Use extra pillows to raise baby to the level of the breast. The baby should be tucked in close to the mother's side and held like a football with the bottom against the back of the chair and the legs up behind mother's arm (Scarborough Breastfeeding Network, 1999; Society of Paediatric Nursing of the Royal College of Nursing, 1998). **The baby's back should be supported with the mother's arm and his shoulders with mother's hand (avoid holding baby's head).**

Illustrations reproduced with the permission of the City of Ottawa.

 RNAO

Appendix G: Latch, Milk Transfer and Effective Breastfeeding

International Lactation Consultant Association (ILCA)
Association of Women's Health, Obstetric and Neonatal Nurses (AWHONN)

Latch (ILCA)

Observe infant for signs of correct latch-on:

- wide opened mouth
- flared lips
- nose, cheeks, and chin touching, or nearly touching, the breast

Milk Transfer (ILCA)

Observe infant for signs of milk transfer:

- sustained rhythmic suck/swallow patterns with occasional pauses
- audible swallowing
- relaxed arms and hands
- moist mouth
- satisfied after feedings

Observe mother for signs of milk transfer:

- strong tugging which is not painful
- thirst
- uterine contractions or increased lochia flow during or after feeding for the first 3-5 days
- milk leaking from the opposite breast while feeding
- relaxation or drowsiness
- breast softening while feeding
- nipple elongated after feeding but not pinched or abraded

90

▶ RNAO

19

Infant Behaviours (AWHONN)

Infant feeding cues:

- Rooting
- Hand-to-mouth movements
- Sucking movements/sounds
- Sucking of fingers or hands
- Opening of mouth in response to tactile stimulation

Transition between behaviour states (sleep to drowsy and quietly alert)

Infant satisfaction/satiety cues including the following:

- During the feeding, a gradual decrease in number of sucks
- Pursed lips, pulling away from the breast and releasing the nipple
- Body relaxed
- Legs extended
- Absence of hunger cues
- Sleep, contented state
- Small amount of milk seen in mouth

Frequency and duration (ILCA)

Frequency and duration of feedings:

- Expect a minimum of 8-12 feedings in 24 hours
- Some infants will breastfeed every 3 hours day and night, others will cluster-feed, feeding every hour for 4-6 feeds then sleeping 4-6 hours
- Expect to feed 15-20 minutes on the first breast and 10-15 minutes on the second but do not be concerned if the infant is satisfied after one breast
- If necessary, wake a sleepy infant for feedings until an appropriate weight gain pattern is established
- Expect feeding frequency to decrease as the infant gets older

Urine (AWHONN)

- One void by 24 hours
- 3 or more voids by next 24 hours
- 6 or more voids by day four

Stool (AWHONN, ILCA)

- One stool by 24 hours (AWHONN)
- 1-2 stools by day 3 (AWHONN)
- 3 or more stools by day 4 (AWHONN)
- Expect bowel movements to change from meconium to a yellow, soft, and watery consistency by day 4 (ILCA)

Weight (ILCA)

- Expect less than 7% weight loss the first week
- Expect return to birth weight by 14 days of age
- Expect weight gain of 4-8 ounces (120 – 240 grams) a week until the infant has doubled birth weight

Ineffective Breastfeeding (ILCA)

- Infant weight loss greater than 7%
- Continued weight loss after day 3
- Less than 3 bowel movements in 24 hours
- Meconium stools after day 4
- Less than 6 wet diapers in 24 hours after day 4
- Infant who is irritable and restless or sleepy and refusing to feed
- No audible swallowing during feedings
- No discernible change in weight or size of breasts and no discernible change in milk volume and composition by 3-5 days
- Persistent or increasingly painful nipples
- Engorgement unrelieved by feeding
- Infant who does not begin to gain weight by day 5
- Infant who has not returned to birth weight by day 14

92

Appendix H:
Immediate Postpartum Decision Tree

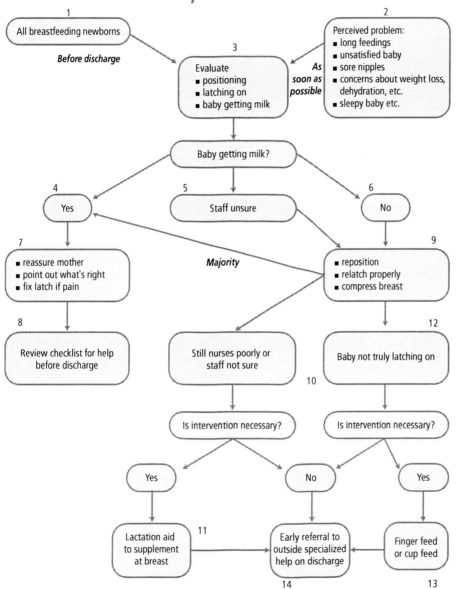

Immediate Postpartum Descision Tree. The same approach can be used to make decisions about breastfeeding at any age of the baby, but may require some modification depending on the age and problems encountered.

Reproduced with permission of Dr. J. Newman, Toronto, Ontario.

Summary of Recommendations

RECOMMENDATION			*LEVEL OF EVIDENCE
Practice Recommendations			
Prevention	1.0	Nurses provide individualized, flexible postpartum care based on the identification of depressive symptoms and maternal preference.	Ia
	2.0	Nurses initiate preventive strategies in the early postpartum period.	Ia
Confirming Depressive Symptoms	3.0	The Edinburgh Postnatal Depression Scale (EPDS) is the recommended self-report tool to confirm depressive symptoms in postpartum mothers.	III
	4.0	The EPDS can be administered anytime throughout the postpartum period (birth to 12 months) to confirm depressive symptoms.	III
	5.0	Nurses encourage postpartum mothers to complete the EPDS by themselves in privacy.	III
	6.0	An EPDS cut-off score greater than 12 may be used to determine depressive symptoms among English-speaking women in the postpartum period. This cut-off criterion should be interpreted cautiously with mothers who: 1) are non-English speaking; 2) use English as a second language, and/or 3) are from diverse cultures.	III
	7.0	The EPDS must be interpreted in combination with clinical judgment to confirm postpartum mothers with depressive symptoms.	III
	8.0	Nurses should provide immediate assessment for self harm ideation/behaviour when a mother scores positive (e.g., from 1 to 3) on the EPDS self-harm item number 10.	IV
Treatment	9.0	Nurses provide supportive weekly interactions and ongoing assessment focusing on mental health needs of postpartum mothers experiencing depressive symptoms.	Ib
	10.0	Nurses facilitate opportunities for the provision of peer support for postpartum mothers with depressive symptoms.	IIb
General	11.0	Nurses facilitate the involvement of partners and family members in the provision of care for postpartum mothers experiencing depressive symptoms, as appropriate.	Ib
	12.0	Nurses promote self-care activities among new mothers to assist in alleviating depressive symptoms during the postpartum period.	IV
	13.0	Nurses consult appropriate resources for current and accurate information before educating mothers with depressive symptoms about psychotropic medications.	IV
Education Recommendations			
	14.0	Nurses providing care to new mothers should receive education on postpartum depression to assist with the confirmation of depressive symptoms and prevention and treatment interventions.	III

*Please refer to page 11 for details regarding "Interpretation of Evidence".

Background Context

The postpartum period is considered a time of increased risk for the onset of mood disorders. Research has shown that a woman is significantly more likely to be admitted to a psychiatric hospital within the first 4 weeks postpartum than at any other time in her life (Kendell, Chambers & Platz,1987; Paffenbarger, 1982; Brockington, Cernick, Schofield, Downing, Francis & Keelan, 1981) and up to 12.5% of all psychiatric hospital admissions of women occur during the postpartum period (Duffy, 1983). Postpartum affective disorders are typically divided into three categories: postpartum blues, postpartum depression, and puerperal psychosis. Postpartum blues is the most common postpartum mood disturbance with prevalence estimates ranging from 30% to 75%. Symptoms, which often begin within the immediate postpartum period and remit within days, include mood lability, irritability, tearfulness, generalized anxiety, and sleep and appetite disturbance. By definition, postpartum blues are transient, mild, time-limited, and do not require treatment other than reassurance (Kennerly & Gath, 1989). Conversely, postpartum psychosis is a very severe depressive episode characterized by the presence of psychotic features. This condition is the most severe and uncommon form of postpartum affective disorders, with rates of 1 to 2 episodes per 1000 deliveries (Kendell et al., 1987). The clinical onset is rapid, with symptoms presenting as early as the first 48 to 72 hours postpartum, and the majority of episodes develop within the first 2 weeks postpartum. The symptoms are typically depressed or elated mood (which can fluctuate rapidly), disorganized behaviour, mood lability, delusions, and hallucinations (Brockington et al., 1981).

Among these conditions is postpartum depression, a nonpsychotic depressive episode beginning in the postpartum period (Cox, Murray & Chapman, 1993; O'Hara,1994; Watson, Elliott, Rugg & Brough, 1984). At present, postpartum depression is not classified as a separate disease; it is diagnosed as part of affective or mood disorders in both the American Psychiatric Association's Diagnostic and Statistical Manual of Mental Disorders (DSM-IV) and the World Health Organization's International Classification of Diseases (ICD-10). According to the DSM-IV, postpartum depression is a depressive disorder with onset within the first 4 weeks postpartum. However to be comprehensive in the literature review and to be able to include the best evidence possible, for this practice guideline, postpartum depression is defined as any depressive episode that occurs within the first year postpartum.

The symptoms of postpartum depression are similar to depression unrelated to childbirth (Wisner, Parry & Piontek, 2002). However, despite these similarities, postpartum depression is frequently exacerbated by other indicators such as low self-esteem, inability to cope, loneliness, feelings of incompetence, and loss of self (Beck, Reynolds & Rutowski, 1992; Mills, Finchilescu & Lea, 1995; Righetti-Veltema, Conne-Perreard, Bousquet & Manzano, 1998; Ritter, Hobfoll, Lavin, Cameron & Hulsizer, 2000). Somatic symptoms of depression, including appetite and sleep disturbances, are often present in women with postpartum depression (Nonacs, & Cohen, 1998). Distinguishing between these depressive symptoms and the supposed 'normal' sequelae of childbirth can make postpartum depression potentially difficult to diagnose (Hostetter & Stowe, 2002). See *Apendix C* for the DSM-IV criteria for a major depressive episode.

Postpartum depression is a major health issue for many women (Affonso, De, Horowitz & Mayberry, 2000). A meta-analysis of 59 studies suggests that approximately 13% of women experience postpartum depression (O'Hara & Swain, 1996) with the inception rate greatest in the first 12 weeks postpartum (Goodman, 2004); these rates do not differ between primiparous and multiparous mothers. While up to 20% of women with postpartum blues will continue to develop postpartum depression (Campbell, Cohn, Flanagan, Popper & Meyers, 1992; O'Hara, Schlechte, Lewis & Wright, 1991b), other women enjoy a period of well-being after delivery followed by a gradual onset of depressive symptoms.

This hidden morbidity has well documented health consequences for the mother, child, and family. While women who have suffered from postpartum depression are twice as likely to experience future episodes of depression over a 5-year period (Cooper & Murray, 1995), infants and children are particularly vulnerable. Untreated postpartum depression can cause impaired maternal-infant interactions (Murray, Fiori-Cowley, Hooper & Cooper, 1996) and negative perceptions of infant behaviour (Mayberry & Affonso, 1993) which have been linked to attachment insecurity (Hipwell, Goossens, Melhuish, & Kumar, 2000; Murray, 1992), and emotional developmental delay (Cogill, Caplan, Alexandra, Robson & Kumar, 1986; Cummings & Davies, 1994; Hipwell et al., 2000; Murray, Sinclair, Cooper, Ducournau, Turner & Stein, 1999; Whiffen & Gotlib, 1989). Marital stress, resulting in separation or divorce (Boyce, 1994; Holden, 1991) is also a reported outcome.

The cause of postpartum depression remains unclear (Cooper & Murray, 1998), with extensive research suggesting a multifactorial aetiology (Ross, Gilbert Evans, Sellers & Romach, 2003). In particular, a variety of biological, psychological, and sociocultural variables likely interact to produce vulnerability to postpartum depression, and the causes or "triggers" of postpartum depression likely vary from woman to woman. Although researchers and health professionals have long speculated that postpartum depression may be linked to the dramatic hormone changes which accompany pregnancy and childbirth, to date no particular hormone has been consistently associated with postpartum depression, nor have any differences in hormones been identified between women with and without postpartum depression (Bloch et al., 2000).

To promote the identification of women experiencing postpartum depression, self-report measures have been developed specifically for use within a postpartum population. Self-report measures are easier and less costly to administer, and do not require the presence of trained specialists. The most well established self-report tool for the identification of postpartum depression is the Edinburgh Postnatal Depression Scale (EPDS), a 10 item self-report measure that has been translated into diverse languages. The EPDS has been rigorously validated against clinical diagnostic interviews (Cox, Holden & Sagovsky, 1987). English- and French-language versions of the EPDS are provided in *Appendices D & E*.

According to epidemiological studies and meta-analyses of predictive studies, the strongest predictors of postpartum depression are: antenatal depression and anxiety, personal and family history of depression, life stress (Beck, 2001; Bernazzani, Saucier, David & Borgeat, 1997; O'Hara & Swain, 1996; O'Hara, Schlechte, Lewis & Varner, 1991a), and the lack of social support (Beck, 2001; Brugha, Sharp, Cooper, Weisender, Britto & Shinkwin, 1998; Cooper & Murray, 1998; Mills et al., 1995; O'Hara & Swain, 1996; O'Hara et al., 1991a; Righetti-Veltema et al., 1998). Two meta-analyses also found a higher risk of postpartum depression among socially disadvantaged women (Beck, 2001; O'Hara & Swain, 1996).

To enhance our understanding of postpartum depression, numerous qualitative research studies have been conducted. To summarize this work, a meta-synthesis of 18 qualitative studies was conducted which identified several overarching themes including: 1) incongruity between expectations and reality of motherhood; 2) spiralling downward; and 3) pervasive loss (Beck, 2002).

Eight of the 18 studies in the meta-synthesis centred on the role that conflicting expectations and experiences of motherhood played in the development of postpartum depression. In particular, women often held unrealistic expectations which were inconsistent with their own experiences as mothers (Mauthner, 1999). This incongruity between expectations and lived experience was described in seven areas: labour and delivery, life with their infants, self as mother, relationship with partners, support from family and friends, life events and physical changes (Berggren-Clive, 1998). When women became disillusioned with motherhood and perceived they had failed to be the 'perfect mother' (Berggren-Clive, 1998), their emotions of despair and sadness started a spiral downward into postpartum depression.

Loss of control was identified as a central theme in 15 out of the 18 studies. Nicolson's (1999) study described how loss of autonomy and time were precursors to feeling out of control due to a lack of time to consider themselves or process their daily experiences. This in turn led to a loss of self-identify, including loss of former sense of self. Women also discussed how postpartum depression led to loss of relationships with their partners, children, and family members (Morgan, Matthey, Barnett & Richardson, 1997). Some women wanted their partners 'to be able to read their minds' and take some initiative in helping them, while others felt that admitting their feelings was a sign of personal inadequacy and failure as a mother (McIntosh, 1993). If they did admit to their feelings, women also risked being misunderstood, rejected, or stigmatized by their loved ones. Women with postpartum depression expressed feelings of being 'different' and 'abnormal' compared to other mothers. They consistently talked about a profound sense of isolation and loneliness. Mothers who were depressed frequently felt discomfort with being around others and believed that no one really understood what they were experiencing (Beck et al., 1992). Consequently, they socially withdrew to escape a potentially critical world (Semprevivo, 1996).

Although qualitative research cannot determine intervention effectiveness, it can provide valuable information such as determining which aspects of care women find most useful. In a variety of studies, mothers who were interviewed have identified the need for health professionals to be aware of and knowledgeable about postpartum depression (Mauthner, 1997). Community education to inform family members about the range of signs and symptoms of postpartum depression was also thought to be beneficial (Ugarizza, 2002). Mothers felt that postpartum depression should be openly discussed in antenatal classes so that women could be better informed. It was thought that this type of discussion may also help to reduce the stigma associated with postpartum depression. In addition, women felt antenatal classes provided an opportunity to develop social support networks (Mauthner, 1997). Mothers also identified 'talking therapies' as an option that should be made available (Chan, Levy, Chung & Lee, 2002). Health professionals who encouraged women to talk about their feelings and who spent time listening were highly valued (Mauthner, 1997). Telephone and web-based support groups have been suggested to assist mothers who are symptomatic in their homes (Ugariizza, 2002). Among ethnospecific populations, mothers felt nurses could foster connections with specific cultural groups by becoming aware of what was available in the community (Nahas, Hillege & Amasheh, 1999). There was also a stated need that nurses understand the cultural beliefs and values of new mothers in order to facilitate culturally sensitive care (Chan et al., 2002; Nahas et al., 1999; Nahas & Amasheh, 1999).

Appendix D: Edinburgh Postnatal Depression Scale (EPDS) English

Reproduction of the EPDS in it's entirety is restricted to print version only. The following is an excerpt of the EPDS for sample purposes.

How are you feeling?

As you have recently had a baby, we would like to know how you are feeling now. Please underline the answer which comes closest to how you have felt in the past 7 days, not just how you feel today. Here is an example, already completed.

I have felt happy:
Yes, most of the time
Yes, some of the time
No, not very often
No, not at all

This would mean: "I have felt happy some of the time during the past week". Please complete the other questions in the same way.

In the past 7 days

1. I have been able to laugh and see the funny side of things:
As much as I always could
Not quite so much now
Definitely not so much now
Not at all

©1987 The Royal College of Psychiatrists. The Edinburgh Postnatal Depression Scale may be photocopied by individual researchers or clinicians for their own use without seeking permission from the publishers. The scale must be copied in full and all copies must acknowledge the following source: Cox, J. L., Holden, J. M. & Sagovsky, R. (1987) Detection of postnatal depression. Development of the 10-item Edinburgh Postnatal Depression Scale. British Journal of Psychiatry, 150, 782-786. Written permission must be obtained from the Royal College of Psychiatrists for copying and distribution to others or for republication (in print, online or by any other medium).

Translations of the scale, and guidance as to its use, may be found in Cox, J. L. & Holden, J. (2003) Perinatal Mental Health: A Guide to the Edinburgh Postnatal Depression Scale. London: Gaskell.

The hard copy of the guideline Interventions for Postpartum Depression is available through the Registered Nurses' Association of Ontario. For more information and an order form, please visit the RNAO website at www.rnao.org/bestpractices.

Appendix F: Administration and Interpretation of the EPDS

The EPDS can be administered to mothers anytime from birth to 52 weeks that have been identified with depressive symptoms either subjectively or objectively.

Instructions for the administration of the EPDS

1. The EPDS may be administered in person.
2. Efforts should be make to have the mother complete the scale by herself, where she feels she can answer the questions honestly.
3. Mother's may need assistance with the EPDS if they have limited reading skills or understanding of the English language.
4. All 10 items on the questionnaire must be completed.
5. The mother or health care professional should underline the response that best describes the mother's feelings in the last week.
6. The EPDS can be administered anytime from 0 to 52 weeks.

Sample lead in statements

Please be as open and honest as possible when answering these questions. It is not easy being a new mother and it is OK to feel unhappy at times. As you have recently had a new baby, we would like to know how you are feeling. Please state the answer which comes closest to how you have felt during the past several days, not just how you are feeling today.

Scoring of the EPDS

Each response is scored 0, 1, 2 or 3 based on the increased severity of the symptoms. Calculate the total score by adding together each of the 10 items.

Interpretation of the EPDS

1. The EPDS score must be considered in combination with the assessment of the health care provider.
2. A score of 13 or greater indicates the presence of depressive symptoms.
3. The score does not reflect the severity of the symptoms.
4. Use caution when interpreting the score of mothers who are non-English speaking and/or use English as a second language or are multicultural.
5. If a mother scores positive (1, 2 or 3) on self-harm item number 10, further assessment should be done immediately for self-harm ideation (refer to *Appendix H & I* for examples of sample questions).
6. Follow agency/institution protocol regarding scores.
7. Remember that the EPDS is only a tool. If your clinical judgment indicates differently than the EPDS continue with the follow up as the assessment indicates.

Translations of the scale, and guidance as to its use, may be found in Cox, J. L. & Holden, J. (2003) Perinatal Mental Health: A Guide to the Edinburgh Postnatal Depression Scale. London: Gaskell.

The tidal model
Barker, Phil, PhD, RN, FRCN
Journal of Psychosocial Nursing & Mental Health Services; Jul 2002; 40, 7;
Nursing & Allied Health Database
pg. 42

The Tidal Model

The Healing Potential of Metaphor Within a Patient's Narrative

Psychiatric nurses traditionally have used different methods of approaching patients in their care. These methods reflected, at least in part, nurses' construction of the phenomena of mental illness (Barker, 1999). These divergent, and at times conflicting, approaches to the delivery of care developed during the past half-century into various theories and models of nursing practice. Increasingly, nurses have acknowledged the need to focus on developing active methods of helping patients participate in their own care, fostering the active collaboration of patients and significant others (Peternelj-Taylor & Hartley, 1993). Peplau's original representation of the therapeutic potential of the nurse-patient relationship currently would appear to have been supplemented by a variety of concerns for the political dynamics of the relationship itself (Barker & Stevenson, 2000).

34

Increasingly, nurses have acknowledged the need to focus on developing active methods of helping patients participate in their own care, fostering the active collaboration of patients and significant others.

Latvala, Janhonen, and Wahlberg (1999) described three distinct methods of helping used by nurses that suggest the dynamics between nurses and patients. Catalytic methods emphasize the use of participatory dialogue and assume the agency responsible for the patient will permit the development of mutual collaboration. Educational methods provide precedence to nurses professional monologues, assuming patients are no more than responsible recipients and the cooperative relationship will be driven primarily by the professionalism of nurses. Finally, confirmatory methods begin with an assumption that mental illness arises from physical causes. This assumption limits the nurse-patient relationship to general discussion, within which the patient is a passive recipient of information. Any cooperation that occurs is within a hierarchical context.

A RESEARCH-BASED MODEL OF MENTAL HEALTH NURSING

The Tidal Model was developed in England between 1995 and 1998 from a series of studies that explored the need for psychiatric nursing (Barker, Jackson, & Stevenson, 1999, p. 273) and, more specifically, the discrete nature of the power relationship between nurses and patients (Barker, Leamy, & Stevenson, 2000). The model acknowledges mental illness can be viewed from differing theoretical perspectives. However, it also appreciates the value of construing mental health problems primarily as problems of living that exist within a human system.

These hypothetical problems delimit the effective functioning of patients at various levels (e.g., intrapersonal, interpersonal, transpersonal, spiritual).

The Tidal Model uses a pragmatic and respectful approach to the identification of problems of living. It echoes the view expressed by Alanen, Lehtinen, and Aaltonen (1991) that patients with serious mental health problems and their families need to be helped to,

conceive of the situation (e.g., admission) as a consequence of the difficulties the patients and those close to them have encountered in their lives, rather than as a mysterious illness the patient has developed as an individual (p. 364).

This attitude emphasizes the centrality of patients and their significant others lived experiences. In its open acknowledgement of the need for mutual understanding between nurses and patients, the Tidal Model may accommodate a variation of the catalytic method described by Latvala et al (1999). In the United Kingdom, this emphasis on mutuality differs markedly from the contemporary popularity of psychosocial and other cognitive-behavioral interventions (e.g., Brooker and Butterworth, 1994) that bridge the confirmatory and educational approaches to helping. Perhaps unwittingly, psychosocial and cognitive-behavioral interventions often openly pledge support to a biomedical construction of mental illness and the inherent problems of living.

Despite emerging participative rhetoric, in most western countries nurse practitioners are aware the medical model is stronger than ever, implying patients need to be treated rather than cared for or with (Dawson, 1997). This suggests any new

JULY 2002

model of mental health nursing practice not only must emphasize the specific need for nursing (Barker et al., 1999), but also should be congruent with patients need for medical and other therapeutic interventions.

The Tidal Model originally was introduced into acute psychiatric care settings (Barker, 1998), but has since developed the concept of a care continuum, with demonstration sites in hospital, community, rehabilitation, and forensic settings. The model emphasizes patients needs for three discrete forms of care critical, transitional, and developmental which represent different hypothetical stages of the care and treatment process. The care continuum spans the hospital-community divide and emphasizes need should be the primary focus for care, rather than the setting within which care is delivered.

Although the model is intended to complement the care and treatment offered by other disciplines, its primary emphasis is the exploration and development of the lived experiences of patients. Methods of revealing and clarifying meanings and values, which patients attach to or associate with problems of living, are emphasized. When appropriate, this exploration extends from the intrapersonal domain through interpersonal conceptions of self and other to address what may be defined, classically, as the religious, mystical, or spiritual dimensions of self-hood (Barker, 2000). However, in every situation, the constructions of the various dimensions of patients experiences of personhood are realized through mutual discussion. Therefore, the completion of each assessment and the development and modification of each care plan becomes an act

Holistic Nursing Assessment

- Details of time, date, and place of the assessment, and who is involved
- General overview of current problems
- Problem origins
- Past problem function (i.e., how this affected me)
- Past emotions
- Developmental history (i.e., how things have changed for me over time)
- History of relationships
- Current emotional state
- Holistic content (i.e., what I think this means)
- Holistic context (i.e., what this says about me as a person)
- Needs, desires, and wishes
- Expectations of the clinical team
- Evaluation of the problem (i.e., rating emotional distress, degree of disruption to life activity, and degree of control over the problem)
- Personal resources
- Resolution of the problem

Figure 1. The Holistic Nursing Assessment is a 6-page document. A copy of the blank format is given to patients, who are invited to choose who (i.e., themselves or interviewing nurses) should write the responses. On completion, nurses copy the original record, which is saved in patients' care plans, and a copy is provided for patients' reference.

of co-creation involving the active collaboration of patients and those involved with their immediate care.

THE TIDAL METAPHOR

In emphasizing the fluid nature of human experience, the Tidal Model borrows from chaos theory (Barker, 1996), recognizing that change, growth, and development occur through small, often barely visible changes, following patterns that paradoxically are consistent in their unpredictability. This provides the basis for the core metaphor water:

Life is a journey undertaken on an ocean of experience. All human development, including the experience of illness and

health, involves discoveries made on a journey across that ocean of experience.

At critical points in the life journey the person may experience storms or even piracy (crisis). At other times the ship may begin to take in water and the person may face the prospect of drowning or shipwreck (breakdown). The person may need to be guided to a safe haven to undertake repairs, or to recover from the trauma (rehabilitation). Only once the ship is made intact, or the person has regained the necessary sea-legs, can the ship set sail again, aiming to put the person back on the life course (recovery).

Unlike normative or adaptational psychiatric models, the

36

OPENING SECTION FROM THE HOLISTIC ASSESSMENT

The holistic assessment helps patients develop the story of how they entered psychiatric care and make sense of the experience. Jack* was readmitted with a diagnosis of paranoid schizophrenia. Having gained Jack's confidence, the interviewing nurse encouraged him to explore the circumstances that led to his admission by asking, "What brought you here?"

I was on the [oil] rigs and was having trouble sleeping. It put me in a bad mood, and the lads started to get on my nerves. In the beginning, I just felt weird. Then it dawned on me that I had gotten radiation sickness from the rig. I know 'they' are targeting me—beaming radiation from the rig. Now my girlfriend has left me, and my sister has got fed up with me talking about it. But I don't tell any of my mates about this. Now I just feel confused. I don't understand what's going on. I don't know what any of this means.

** Name changed to protect anonymity.*

Figure 2.

Tidal Model holds few assumptions about the proper course of patients lives. Instead, it focuses on the type of support patients believe they need to live good lives. The Tidal Model recognizes life experiences associated with mental illness are invariably described in metaphorical terms (Barker, 2000).

Patients who experience life crises are metaphorically in deep water and risk drowning, or feel they have been thrown onto the rocks. Patients who have experienced trauma, such as injury or abuse, or those with more enduring life problems (e.g., repeated breakdowns, hospitalizations, or loss of freedom through compulsory detention), often report loss of sense of self akin to the trauma associated with piracy. In such situations, patients need a sophisticated form of lifesaving (i.e., psychiatric rescue) followed, at an appropriate interval, by the type of developmental work necessary to engender true recovery. This may take the form of crisis intervention in the community or the safe haven of inpatient settings. After the rescue is complete (i.e., psychiatric nursing), the emphasis switches to the type of help needed for patients to get back on course, returning to a meaningful life in the community (i.e., mental health nursing).

The model assumes the practical focus of psychiatric and mental health nursing differs. The former requires supportive, and often dramatic, interventions in which patients are vulnerable and potentially dependent. The latter emphasizes an egalitarian relationship, within which collaborative and empowering interventions have the potential to facilitate personal growth and discovery.

The Tidal Model is predicated on the use of a range of discrete holistic (exploratory) and focused (risk) assessments, each of which generates patient-centered interventions that emphasize patients extant resources and capacity for finding solutions. The templates for assessment and intervention contained within the model act as a springboard for creative exploration of the need for nursing (Barker et al., 1999), rather than delimiting nurses practice through the exercise of tight protocols. By acknowledging the need for a continuously flexible response to patients, the Tidal Model also recognizes the inherently chaotic nature of human behavior and experience (Barker, 1996).

LIFE AS NARRATIVE

The Tidal Model assumes patients are their narratives (MacIntyre, 1981). Patients sense of self and world of experiences, including experience of others, are inextricably tied to the life story and the various meanings generated within it. The Tidal Model constructs a narrative-based form of practice (Barker & Kerr, 2001). This differs markedly from some contemporary forms of evidence-based practice. The former is always about particular human instances, whereas the latter is based on the behavior of populations whose elements are assumed to be equivalent. More important, the narrative focus of the Tidal Model is not concerned with unraveling the causative course of patients problems of living, but aims to use the experience of patients journey and its associated meanings to chart the next step to be taken on the life journey.

As part of this conjoint exploration of patients world of experience, the assessment record is written entirely in patients voices, rather than translated into a third person account or professional language (Figure 1). Nurses and patients co-create a narrative account of the patients world of experience, including the identification of what patients believe they need in terms of nursing interventions and holding the promise of what needs to happen to meet that need (Figure 2).

Whatever the clinical presentation, the Tidal Model provides precedence to the story because this is the location for enactment of patients lives. It is the theater of experience in which reflection and discussion result in a contemporaneous script editing. The caring process begins and ends here because all patients express a need to develop (i.e., create) a coherent account of what has happened and currently is happening to them, in light of their personal experience. This account is most meaningful when framed in the patients vernacular, illustrated by the metaphorical language drawn from patients history and sociocultural context.

In the course of mental health care and treatment, it is commonplace for nurses to note that patients change their stories. This is a reflection of how consideration of the past in light of the present serves notice that patients also are involved in creating the future, which is imaginary. Therefore, it is foolish to talk of some putative true story because this is no more than a pattern of context or agency. Instead, nurses aim to help patients develop a story, which takes into account how patients make sense of life events, including the process of care, as and when they occur (Figure 3).

In translating the metaphor of the script edit into care planning language, the model proposes patients should be assessed only once (holistically) during each period of contact with the service. This assessment leads directly to the development of the first care plan, which is reviewed and revised daily with patients who are in residential care, tailoring and adapting the processes of care to fit what might be small, but significant, changes in patients presentations. The story from the first holistic assessment becomes the opening chapter of the story of the current episode of care. This is written conjointly, page by page, and is closed only when patients are ready to make the transition to home or to a new care setting.

EMPOWERMENT

The experience of mental illness is inherently disempowering. Although services often are described as offering mental health interventions, invariably these focus only on limiting the personal and interpersonal damage resulting from problems of living. Consequently, psychiatric care and treatment can compound the original disempowerment scenario of illness.

The Tidal Model attempts to directly address the most common form of disempowerment, which is the failure to afford a proper hearing to the story of problems of living. Traditionally, the medical model has deflected attention away from the lived experience, translating this unique, subjective account into the paralanguage of medicine. Many psychological models or psychotherapies do the same thing, reframing the lived experience as one kind of psychological schema or another. The personal account thus is reduced to the level of its apparently commonly occurring parts. This view is not a condemnation of psychiatric or psychotherapeutic diagnosis per se, but is merely an acknowledgement of the limitations of this

Although the model is intended to complement the care and treatment offered by other disciplines, its primary emphasis is the exploration and development of the lived experiences of patients.

47

38

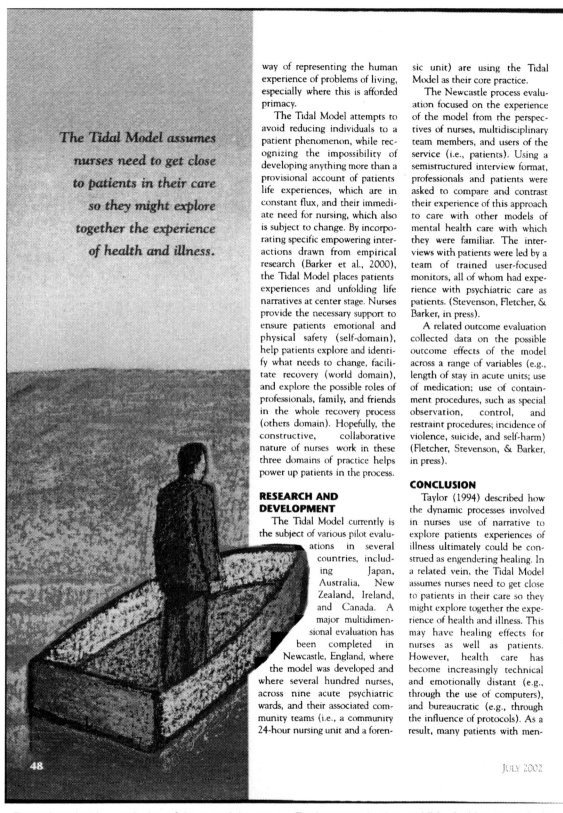

The Tidal Model assumes nurses need to get close to patients in their care so they might explore together the experience of health and illness.

way of representing the human experience of problems of living, especially where this is afforded primacy.

The Tidal Model attempts to avoid reducing individuals to a patient phenomenon, while recognizing the impossibility of developing anything more than a provisional account of patients life experiences, which are in constant flux, and their immediate need for nursing, which also is subject to change. By incorporating specific empowering interactions drawn from empirical research (Barker et al., 2000), the Tidal Model places patients experiences and unfolding life narratives at center stage. Nurses provide the necessary support to ensure patients emotional and physical safety (self-domain), help patients explore and identify what needs to change, facilitate recovery (world domain), and explore the possible roles of professionals, family, and friends in the whole recovery process (others domain). Hopefully, the constructive, collaborative nature of nurses work in these three domains of practice helps power up patients in the process.

RESEARCH AND DEVELOPMENT

The Tidal Model currently is the subject of various pilot evaluations in several countries, including Japan, Australia, New Zealand, Ireland, and Canada. A major multidimensional evaluation has been completed in Newcastle, England, where the model was developed and where several hundred nurses, across nine acute psychiatric wards, and their associated community teams (i.e., a community 24-hour nursing unit and a foren-

sic unit) are using the Tidal Model as their core practice.

The Newcastle process evaluation focused on the experience of the model from the perspectives of nurses, multidisciplinary team members, and users of the service (i.e., patients). Using a semistructured interview format, professionals and patients were asked to compare and contrast their experience of this approach to care with other models of mental health care with which they were familiar. The interviews with patients were led by a team of trained user-focused monitors, all of whom had experience with psychiatric care as patients. (Stevenson, Fletcher, & Barker, in press).

A related outcome evaluation collected data on the possible outcome effects of the model across a range of variables (e.g., length of stay in acute units; use of medication; use of containment procedures, such as special observation, control, and restraint procedures; incidence of violence, suicide, and self-harm) (Fletcher, Stevenson, & Barker, in press).

CONCLUSION

Taylor (1994) described how the dynamic processes involved in nurses use of narrative to explore patients experiences of illness ultimately could be construed as engendering healing. In a related vein, the Tidal Model assumes nurses need to get close to patients in their care so they might explore together the experience of health and illness. This may have healing effects for nurses as well as patients. However, health care has become increasingly technical and emotionally distant (e.g., through the use of computers), and bureaucratic (e.g., through the influence of protocols). As a result, many patients with men-

ARCHIE'S STORY

Archie, a 20-year-old man with paranoid psychosis, tried to set fire to himself in an intensive psychiatric care unit and burnt down the unit in the process. Considered high risk, Archie was transferred to another secure unit where the admitting nurse helped him explore the wider context of his current problems, beginning with the circumstances of his transfer:

Nurse: So, Archie, what brought you here?

Archie: (very agitated) They told me to do it. They said it was the only way . . . . I got a sign, lots of signs, in the stars . . . like black everywhere . . . the only way, I mean they did. They said, 'It's the only way.'

Nurse: Uh huh, they did. Can you tell me who they are, Archie?

Archie: I dunno. I mean I dunno who they are. But they told me.

Nurse: I see. And when did you first become aware of them?

Archie: They were like voices . . . I keep hearing them, talking . . . lots of talking. Burn, burn, boy, burn! I, oh, I don't remember when they first came . . . long time ago. Been a long time.

The nurse invited Archie to talk more about the voices and asked Archie to "help me understand what is happening." She also invited him to stop and rest at points, and to decide what bits of the story he wanted written down to help the team understand what was happening with him. As the nurse listened carefully, using his language, pacing herself to Archie's rhythm,

Archie gradually became calmer and more coherent. The nurse then paraphrased Archie's story, so far.

Nurse: So, let me see if I have understood what you have been saying, Archie. Just stop me if I have misunderstood you.

The nurse paraphrased Archie's story and invited him to "tell me what you think all of this means." Almost without hesitation, Archie replied.

Archie: It means I have a chance to be reborn.

Nurse: Reborn? Can you tell me more about that?

Archie: Yeah, like, make a fresh start, you know, begin again. Have a clean sheet, a fresh start, a blank page.

Nurse: This is important, yes?

Archie: I guess. I guess I messed up, big time. That's what they kept telling me. I guess they knew.

Nurse: So, what do you think that says about you as a person?

Archie: Well . . . maybe . . . I'm not so bad after all. I mean, like, getting a second chance and all that. Maybe. Just maybe.

In a more traditional interview, as soon as Archie began talking about the voices and had provided his history, the nurse might have moved precipitately toward identifying risk management strategies, such as medication and special observations. Archie was clearly at high risk of harming himself and others. However, by exploring, rather than closing down, the narrative, the nurse began to involve Archie in what needed to be done to help him.

Figure 3. Archie's Story.

tal health problems, as well as some professionals, have called for a reemphasis on the importance of the human relationship between patient and caregiver (Newnes, Holmes, & Dunn, 1999).

Despite major developments occurring in health, the practice of psychiatric and mental health nursing appears to be predicated on a type of confession of trauma and physical and emotional vul-nerability within an intimate conversation (i.e., the assessment/therapeutic dialogue). However, postmodern, secular society increasingly appears reluctant to acknowledge the potential for anything more than a materialistic construction of mental health problems. The exploration of meanings patients attribute to the experiences in their lives is one definition of spirituality (Barker, 2000). As such, it is possible that for some patients, the process of working with the narrative of their problems of living ultimately might be construed as a form of spiritual inquiry.

Despite the continued popularity of nursing as a human intervention in various surveys of psychiatric staff (Rogers, Pilgrim, & Lacey, 1993), the functional relationship between nurses' ministrations and any

40

benefit perceived by patients remains unclear. The Tidal Model may represent another conceptual framework through which nurses might explore Nightingale's proposition that their primary role is not to cure or heal directly, but rather to organize the conditions under which patients may be healed by nature or God.

REFERENCES

Alanen, Y., Lehtinen, K., & Aaltonen, J. (1991). Need-adapted treatment of new schizophrenic patients: Experience and results of the Turku project. *Acta Psychiatrica Scandanavica, 83,* 363-372.

Barker, P. (1998). It's time to turn the tide. *Nursing Times, 94*(46), 70-72.

Barker, P. (1999). *The philosophy and practice of psychiatric nursing.* Edinburgh: Churchill Livingstone.

Barker, P. (2000). Working with the metaphor of life and death. *Journal of Medical Ethics, 26,* 97-102.

Barker, P., Jackson, S., & Stevenson, C. (1999). What are psychiatric nurses needed for? Developing a theory of essential nursing practice. *Journal of Psychiatric and Mental Health Nursing, 6,* 273-282.

Barker, P., & Kerr, B. (2001). *The process of psychotherapy: A journey of discovery.* Oxford: Butterworth-Heinemann.

Barker, P., Leamy, M., & Stevenson, C. (2000). The philosophy of empowerment. *Mental Health Nursing, 20*(9), 8-12.

Barker, P., & Stevenson, C. (2000). *The construction of power and authority in psychiatry.* Oxford: Butterworth Heinemann.

Barker, P.J. (1996). Chaos and the way of Zen: Psychiatric nursing and the 'uncertainty principle.' *Journal of Psychiatric and Mental Health Nursing, 3,* 235-243.

Brooker, C., & Butterworth, T. (1994). Training in psychosocial intervention: The impact on the role of community psychiatric nursing. *Journal of Advanced Nursing, 18,* 583-590.

Dawson, P.J. (1997). A reply to Kevin Gournay's 'Schizophrenia: A review of the contemporary literature and implications for mental health nursing theory, practice and education.' *Journal of Psychiatric and Mental Health Nursing, 4,* 1-7.

Fletcher, E., Stevenson, C., & Barker, P. (in press). Judgement days: Developing an evaluation for an innovative nursing model. *Journal of Psychiatric and Mental Health Nursing.*

Latvala, E., Janhonen, S., & Wahlberg, K.E. (1999). Patient initiatives during the assessment and planning of psychiatric nursing in a hospital environment. *Journal of Advanced Nursing, 21,* 64-71.

MacIntyre, A. (1981). *After virtue.* Notre Dame, IN: Notre Dame University Press.

Newnes, C., Holmes, G., & Dunn, C. (1999). *This is madness: A critical look at psychiatry and the future of mental health services.* Ross-on-Wye, England: PCCS Books.

Peternelj-Taylor, C.A., & Hartley, V.L. (1993). Living with mental illness: Professional/family collaboration. *Journal of Psychosocial Nursing and Mental Health Services, 31*(3), 23-28.

Rogers, A., Pilgrim, D., & Lacey, B. (1993). *Experiencing psychiatry.* London: Macmillan.

Stevenson, C., Fletcher, E., & Barker, P. (in press). A user-focused evaluation of the Tidal Model. *Journal of Psychiatric and Mental Health Nursing.*

Taylor, B.J. (1994). *Being human: Ordinariness in nursing.* Melbourne, Australia: Churchill Livingstone.

Dr. Barker is Professor of Psychiatric Nursing Practice, University of Newcastle, Department of Psychiatry, Royal Victoria Infirmary, Newcastle Upon Tyne, England.

Address correspondence to Phil Barker, PhD, RN, FRCN, Professor of Psychiatric Nursing Practice, University of Newcastle, Department of Psychiatry, Royal Victoria Infirmary, Newcastle Upon Tyne NE1 4LP, England; e-mail: p.j.barker@ncl.ac.uk

COPING WITH

RECOVERY AS A JOURNEY OF THE HEART

▽

PATRICIA DEEGAN

───

PATRICIA DEEGAN, PH.D., IS A
CONSULTANT WITH THE NATIONAL
EMPOWERMENT CENTER
IN LAWRENCE. MA.

───

THIS ARTICLE WAS ORIGINALLY
PRESENTED AT A CONFERENCE
CO-SPONSORED BY THE ALLIANCE FOR
THE MENTALLY ILL OF MASSACHUSETTS
& THE DEPARTMENT OF MENTAL
HEALTH OF MASSACHUSETTS
CURRICULUM AND TRAINING
COMMITTEE. AND HELD AT THE
MASSACHUSETTS STATE HOUSE
ON MAY 10. 1995.

I would like to thank you for this opportunity to speak with you today. I am especially pleased to be speaking to so many faculty and field supervisors. Your task is very important. You are teaching students who will become tomorrow's mental health professionals. The message I would like to bring to you today is that it is not enough to merely teach them facts and figures and knowledge. We must also help students to seek wisdom.

There is a difference between knowledge and wisdom. The etymological root of the word *knowledge* comes from the Middle English, *to recognize*. And indeed students in the various mental health related disciplines are required to recognize and to master a specific field of knowledge. They are required to know how to conduct empirical inquiry, to formulate findings, to contribute to theoretical models, to learn clinical skills, etc. However students are not required to seek wisdom. Wisdom comes from the Greek *eidos* and *idein* which means to see the form or essence of that which is. Thus most students emerge from their studies full of knowledge or the ability to recognize things, but they lack wisdom or the ability to see the form or essence of that which is.

For example, when we teach our students about the heart we teach them that the heart is a pump; a type of organic machine with valves and chambers. And indeed, in time they learn to recognize the anatomical heart in all its detail. After successfully passing their final anatomy exam we say, This student knows about the heart. But in wisdom we would have to doubt this statement.

Wisdom would seek the form or essence of the heart. In wisdom we would see that the anatomical heart, which we have given our students to study, is nobody's heart. It is a heart that could belong to anybody and therefore it belongs to nobody. Wisdom would have us understand that there is another heart. There is a heart that we know about long before we are taught that the heart is a pump. I am speaking here of the heart that can break; the heart that grows weary; the hardened heart; the heartless one; the cold heart; the heart that aches; the heart that stands still; the heart that leaps with joy; and the one who has lost heart. Wisdom demands that we teach students of the human sciences about the essence of this heart. The human heart. Not the pump that beats in any body but the one that lives in my body and in your body.

In a similar fashion we pass on knowledge about mental illness. Students emerge from school with knowledge about neurotransmitters and schizophrenics and bipolars and borderlines and multiples and OCDs. They become experts in recognizing illness and disease. But this is where we so often fail them. We fail them because we have not taught them to seek wisdom to move beyond mere recognition in order to seek the essence of what is. We have failed to teach them to reverence the human being who exists prior to and in spite of the diagnosis we have placed upon them. Just as the generic, anatomical heart does not exist, neither does the schizophrenic or the multiple or the bipolar exist outside of a generic textbook. What exists, in the truly existential sense, is not an illness or disease. What exists is a human being and wisdom demands that we see and reverence this human being before all else. Wisdom demands that we whole heartedly enter into a relationship with human beings in order to understand them and their experience. Only then are we able to help in a way that is experienced as helpful.

Those of us who have been labeled with mental illness are first and foremost human beings. We are more than the sum of the electrochemical activity of our brain. Our hearts are not merely pumps. Our hearts are as real and as vulnerable as valuable as yours are. We are people. We are people who have experienced great distress and who face the challenge of recovery.

The concept of recovery is rooted in the simple yet profound realization that people who have been diagnosed with mental illness are human beings. Like a pebble tossed into the center of a still pool, this simple fact radiates in ever larger ripples until every corner of academic and applied mental health science and clinical practice are affected.

Those of us who have been diagnosed are not objects to be acted upon. We are fully human subjects who can act and in acting, change our situation. We are human beings and we can speak for ourselves. We have a voice and can learn to use it. We have the right to be heard and listened to. We can become self determining. We can take a stand toward what is distressing to us and need not be passive victims of an illness. We can become experts in our own journey of recovery.

The goal of recovery is not to get mainstreamed. We don't want to be mainstreamed. We say let the mainstream become a wide stream that has room for all of us and leaves no one stranded on the fringes.

The goal of the recovery process is not to become normal. The goal is to embrace our human vocation of becoming more deeply, more fully human. The goal is not normalization. The goal is to become the unique, awesome, never to be repeated human being that we are called to be. The philosopher Martin Heidegger said that to be human means to be a question in search of an answer. Those of us who have been labeled with mental illness are not de facto excused from this most fundamental task of becoming human. In fact, because many of us have experienced our lives and dreams shattering in the wake of mental illness, one of the most essential challenges that faces us is to ask, who can I become and why should I say yes to life?

To be human means to be a question in search of an answer. However, many of us who have been psychiatrically labeled have received powerful messages from professionals who in effect tell us that by virtue of our diagnosis the question of our being has already been answered and our futures are already sealed. For instance, I can remember such a time during my third hospitaliza-

tion. I was 18 years old. I asked the psychiatrist I was working with, What's wrong with me? He said, You have a disease called chronic schizophrenia. It is a disease that is like diabetes. If you take medications for the rest of your life and avoid stress, then maybe you can cope. And as he spoke these words I could feel the weight of them crushing my already fragile hopes and dreams and aspirations for my life. Even some 22 years later, those words still echo like a haunting memory that does not fade.

Today I understand why this experience was so damaging to me. In essence the psychiatrist was telling me that my life, by virtue of being labeled with schizophrenia, was already a closed book. He was saying that my future had already been written. The goals and dreams that I aspired to were mere fantasies according to his prognosis of doom. When the future has been closed off in this way, then the present loses its orientation and becomes nothing but a succession of unrelated moments. Today I know that this psychiatrist had little wisdom at that time. He merely had some knowledge and recognized me as the schizophrenic who had been handed down through the generations by Kraeplin and Bleuler. He did not see me. He saw an illness. We must urge our students to seek wisdom, to move beyond mere recognition of illness, and to wholeheartedly encounter the human being who comes for help. It is imperative that we teach students that relationship is the most powerful tool they have in working with people.

Beyond the goals of recovery, there is the question of the process of recovery. How does one enter into the journey of recovery? Today I would like to begin a conceptualization of recovery as a journey of the heart. We will begin in that place where many people find themselves; in that place of being hard of heart and not caring anymore.

Prior to becoming active participants in our own recovery process, many of us find ourselves in a time of great apathy and indifference. It is a time of having a hardened heart. Of not caring anymore. It is a time when we feel ourselves to be among the living dead: alone, abandoned, and adrift on a dead and silent sea without course or bearing. If I turn my gaze back I can see myself at seventeen years old, diagnosed with chronic schizophrenia, drugged on Haldol and sitting in a chair. As I conjure the image the first thing I can see are that girl's yellow, nicotine stained fingers. I can see her shuffled, stiff, drugged walk. Her eyes do not dance. The dancer has collapsed and her eyes are dark and they stare endlessly into nowhere.

People come and people go. People urge her to do things to help herself but her heart is hard and she cares about nothing except sleeping, sitting, and smoking cigarettes. Her day consists of this: At eight in the morning she forces herself out of bed. In a drugged haze she sits in a chair, the same chair every day. She begins smoking cigarettes.

Cigarette after cigarette. Cigarettes mark the passing of time. Cigarettes are proof that time is passing and that fact, at least, is a relief. From 9 A.M. to noon she sits and smokes and stares. Then she has lunch. At 1 P.M. she goes back to bed to sleep until 3 P.M. At that time she returns to the chair and sits and smokes and stares. Then she has dinner. Then she returns to the chair at 6 P.M. Finally it is 8 o'clock in the evening, the long awaited hour, the time to go back to bed and to collapse into a drugged and dreamless sleep.

This scenario unfolds the next day and the next and then the next, until the months pass by in numbing succession, marked only by the next cigarette and the next …

During this time people would try to motivate me. I remember people trying

> "GIVING UP WAS NOT A PROBLEM, IT WAS A SOLUTION. IT WAS A SOLUTION BECAUSE IT PROTECTED ME FROM WANTING ANYTHING. IF I DIDN'T WANT ANYTHING, THEN IT COULDN'T BE TAKEN AWAY. IF I DIDN'T TRY, THEN I WOULDN'T HAVE TO UNDERGO ANOTHER FAILURE. IF I DIDN'T CARE, THEN NOTHING COULD HURT ME AGAIN. MY HEART BECAME HARDENED."

to make me participate in food shopping on Wednesday or to help bake bread or to go on a boat ride. But nothing anyone did touched me or moved me or mattered to me. I had given up. Giving up was a solution for me. The fact that I was unmotivated was seen as a problem by the people who worked with me. But for me, giving up was not a problem, it was a solution. It was a solution because it protected me from

wanting anything. If I didn't want anything, then it couldn't be taken away. If I didn't try, then I wouldn't have to undergo another failure. If I didn't care, then nothing could hurt me again. My heart became hardened. The spring came and went and I didn't care. Holidays came and went and I didn't care. My friends went off to college and started new lives and I didn't care. A friend whom I had once loved very much came over to visit me and I didn't care. I remember sitting and smoking and saying almost nothing. And as soon as the clock struck 8, I remember interrupting my friend in mid sentence and telling her to go home because I was going to bed. Without even saying goodbye I headed for my bed. My heart was hard. I didn't care about anything.

I trust that the picture I am painting here is familiar to many of us. We recognize this picture of apathy, withdrawal, isolation, and lack of motivation. But if we go beyond mere recognition in search of wisdom we must dig deeper. What is this apathy, indifference, hardness of heart that keeps so many people in a mode of survival and prevents them from actively entering into their own journey of recovery? Is it merely the negative symptoms of schizophrenia? I think not. I believe that becoming hard of heart and not caring anymore is a strategy that desperate people who are at the brink of losing hope, adopt in order to remain alive.

Hope is not just a nice sounding euphemism. Hope and biological life are inextricably intertwined. Martin Seligman's (1975) work in the field of learned helpless offers us great insight into the chiasmic intertwining of hope and biological life. He sights two examples. The first is a published report by Dr. H. M. Lefcourt (1973):

> This writer witnessed one such case of death due to a loss of will within a psychiatric hospital. A female pa-

tient who had remained in a mute state for nearly 10 years was shifted to a different floor of her building along with her floor mates, while her unit was being redecorated. The third floor of this psychiatric unit where the patient in question had been living was known among the patients as the chronic, hopeless floor. In contrast, the first floor was most commonly occupied by patients who held privileges, including the freedom to come and go on the hospital grounds and to the surrounding streets. In short, the first floor was an exit ward from which patients could anticipate discharge fairly rapidly. All patients who were temporarily moved from the third floor were given medical examinations prior to the move, and the patient in question was judged to be in excellent medical health though still mute and withdrawn. Shortly after moving to the first floor, this chronic psychiatric patient surprised the ward staff by becoming socially responsive such that within a two week period she ceased being mute and was actually becoming gregarious. As fate would have it, the redecoration of the third floor unit was soon completed and all previous residents were returned to it. Within a week after she had been returned to the hopeless unit, this patient…collapsed and died. The subsequent autopsy revealed no pathology of note and it was whimsically suggested at the time that the patient had died of despair. (p.182–183)

The second example is that of an army medical officer named Major F. Harold Kushner. Major Kushner was shot down over North Vietnam and he was interned in a prisoner of war camp from 1968 to 1973. Here is how Dr. Seligman relates the story:

When Major Kushner arrived a First Camp in January 1968, Robert has already been captive for two years. He was a rugged and intelligent corporal from a crack marine unit, austere, stoic, and oblivious to pain and suffering. He was 24 years old…Like the rest of the men, he was down to a weight of ninety pounds and was forced to make long, shoeless treks daily with ninety pounds of manioc root on his back. He never griped…Despite malnutrition and terrible skin disease, he remained in very good physical and mental health. The cause of his relatively fine shape was clear to (Major) Kushner. Robert was convinced that he would soon be released. The Viet Cong had made it a practice to release, as examples, a few men who had co operated with them… Robert had done so, and the camp commander had indicated that he was next in line for release, to come in six months.… .

The [designated] month came and went, and [Robert] began to sense a change in the guards' attitude toward him. Finally it dawned on him that he had been deceived, that he wasn't going to be released. He stopped working and showed signs of severe depression: he refused food and lay on his bed in a fetal position, sucking his thumb. His fellow prisoners tried to bring him around. They hugged him, babied him and, when this didn't work, tried to bring him out of his stupor with their fists. He defecated and urinated in bed. After a few weeks, it was apparent to Kushner that Robert was moribund: although otherwise his gross physical shape was still better than most of the others, he was dusky and cyanotic. In the early hours of a November morning he lay dying in Kushner's arms. For the first time in days his eyes focused and he spoke: Doe, Post Office Box 161, Texarkana, Texas. Mom, Dad, I love you very much… Within seconds, he was dead. (p. 168)

Seligman (1975, p. 168)) goes on to comment: Hope of release sustained Robert. When he gave up hope, when he believed that all his efforts had failed and would continue to fail, he died. Can a psychological state be lethal? I believe it can. When animals and men learn that their actions are futile and that there is no hope, they become more susceptible to death. Conversely, the belief in control over the environment can prolong life.

To paraphrase I would say that when those of us with psychiatric disabilities come to believe that all of our efforts are futile; when we experience that we have no control over our environment; when nothing we do seems to matter or to make the situation better; when we follow the treatment teams' instructions and achieve their treatment goals for us and still no placement opens up in the community for us; when we try one medication after another after another and none of them seem to be of any help; when we find that staff do not listen to us and that they make all of the major decisions for us; when staff decide where we will live, with whom we will live; under what rules we will live, how we will spend our money, if we will be allowed to spend our money, when we will have to leave the group home, and at what time we will be allowed back into it, etc. etc. etc., then a deep sense of hopelessness, of despair begins to settle over the human heart. And in an effort to avoid the biologically disastrous effects of profound hopelessness, people with psychiatric disabilities do what other people do. We grow hard of heart and attempt to stop caring. It is safer to become helpless then to become hopeless.

Of course, the great danger is that staff will fail to recognize the intensity of the existential struggle that the person who is hard of heart is struggling with. The danger is that the staff will simply say,

46

Oh, this person just has a lot of negative signs and symptoms and that's a poor prognosis and we mustn't expect much from this person. Or staff may become judgmental and dismiss us as simply being lazy and unmotivated. Or the staff may succumb to their own despair and simply write us off as being low functioning.

It is imperative that the instructors and field trainers of the next generation of mental health professionals help today's students to avoid these pitfalls. It is imperative that students be helped to understand that being hard hearted and not caring are highly motivated, adaptive strategies used by desperate people who are at great risk of losing hope. We must help students understand and empathize with the deep existential struggle that is at the heart of this dark night of despair.

There are a number of things I tell students about how to work with people who appear to be hard of heart, apathetic, and unmotivated. First I help the student understand the behavior in terms of its existential significance. I want the student to grasp the magnitude of what it is they are asking a person to risk when they ask them to start to care about something again. I want them to understand that under the hardened heart lies the breaking heart. How much suffering, how much loss can a human heart hold before it breaks? It is not a crazy thing to try to protect such a vulnerable heart. Students must be helped to honor the strategy of giving up and to understand that perhaps that person shall never risk again. In any case, it is only the person whom we are trying to help who has the power to take the risk, to care about something as simple perhaps as caring enough to put a poster on their bedroom wall, or caring enough to wear some new clothes or to try a job placement. These may seem like small things but if we understand their full

existential significance, such acts are small steps toward caring, toward admitting that I just might want to participate in the human community again.

Secondly, I ask students to suspend their perception of people as chronic mental patients and to try to see the individual as a hero. I ask them, could you have survived what this individual has survived? Perhaps this individual has done what you could not do. Perhaps they are not weak and fragile sick people. Perhaps those of us with psychiatric disabilities are incredibly strong and have fiercely tenacious spirits. Could you live on $530 a month and cope with a disability at the same time? If a student can momentarily drop out of his or her distanced professional posture and, in true humility, come to see a person with a psychiatric disability as a hero who has survived, then I say there is a good prognosis for that student That student has a chance of being human hearted while working in the human services and this is no small accomplishment.

Finally, I try to help students understand that although they do not have the power to change or motivate the person with a psychiatric disability who is hard of heart, they do have the power to change the environment, including the human interactive environment, in which that person is surviving. When working with a person with a psychiatric disability who is hard of heart, who has given up and who is motivated not to care anymore, we must understand that this is a person who feels they have no power. They experience all the power to be in the hands of others. They experience what psychologists call an external locus of control. For such people it is imperative to create an environment in which there are choices to be made. I am speaking here, not of forced choice such as either you take your medications or you go back to the

hospital (this is little more than coercion), but of real choices. I am speaking here of all types of choices, from small concerns such as what flavor ice cream you want, to what coffee shop you want to go to, to what kind of vocational goals you might want to pursue, etc.

The person with a hardened heart will reject, reject, and reject again these invitations to choose. However the staff must not fall into despair, feel like their efforts are futile, grow hard of heart, and stop caring themselves. If they do this, then they are doing exactly what the person with a psychiatric disability is doing. Staff must avoid this trap. They must do what the person cannot yet do. Staff must role model hope and continue to offer options and choices even if they are rejected over and over again.

Additionally, environments must include opportunities for people to have accurate information. Information is power and information sharing is power sharing. People who feel powerless can increase their sense of self efficacy by having access to information. People who feel powerless also feel that what they say does not matter. Taking the time to listen to people and to help them find their own unique voice is important. Having a voice in developing rules, as well as having a say in the hiring and evaluation of staff, are important ways of exercising a voice that for too long has been silenced. Finally, it is important to have other people with psychiatric disabilities working as paid staff. Role models provide hope that maybe I, too, can break out of this hardened heart and begin to care again. People who are defending themselves against the possibly lethal effects of profound hopelessness must see that there is a way out and that actions they take can inch them ever closer to their desired goal. They need to see that the quality of life can get better for people who have been similarly diagnosed. They need to see that there are opportunities for improving their situation. That is why hiring people with psychiatric disabilities as mental health professionals and staff is so important. It is also why exposure to peer support, self help and mutual support are so important.

Choice, options, information, role models, being heard, developing and exercising a voice, opportunities for bettering one's life— these are the features of a human interactive environment that support the transition from not caring to caring, from surviving to becoming an active participant in one's own recovery process. Creating such environments are the skills that tomorrow's mental health professionals must master.

As for myself, I cannot remember a specific moment when I turned that corner from surviving to becoming an active participant in my own recovery process. My efforts to protect my breaking heart by becoming hard of heart and not caring about anything lasted for a long time. One thing I can recall is that the people around me did not give up on me. They kept inviting me to do things. I remember one day, for no particular reason, saying yes to helping with food shopping. All I would do was push the cart. But it was a beginning. And truly, it was through small steps like these that I slowly began to discover that I could take a stand toward what was distressing to me.

I know that anger, especially angry indignation, played a big role in that transition. When that psychiatrist told me the best I could hope for was to take my medications, avoid stress and cope, I became enraged. (However, I was smart enough to keep my angry indignation to myself because rule #1 is never get enraged in a psychiatrist's office if you're labeled with chronic schizophrenia!) I also remember that just after that visit I made up my mind to become a doctor. I was so outraged at the things

that had been done to me against my will in the hospital as well as the things I saw happen to other people, that I decided that I wanted to get a powerful degree and have enough credentials to run a healing place myself. In effect, I had a survivor mission that I felt passionately about.

I was also careful not to share my newfound aspiration with anyone. Imagine what my psychiatrist would have said to me if I had announced at age 18, having virtually flunked out of high school, with a combined GRE score of under 800, with a diagnosis of chronic schizophrenia, that I was planning on getting my Ph.D. in clinical psychology. Delusions of grandeur! But in essence that is precisely what I did. Starting with one course in English Composition at the local community college I slowly made my way. Dragging my textbooks into the mental hospital with me or trying to read with double vision due to Prolixin, I inched my way forward. I had a strong spirituality that really helped. I had a strong therapeutic alliance with a psychotherapist. I lived with really weird hippies who had tolerance for lots of weird behavior including my psychotic episodes. After some experimenting in my early teens, I somehow intuited that drugs and alcohol were bad news for me and I did not use them even though the people around me did. In retrospect, I know this was a wise decision. I read tons of books about healing and psychopathology and personality theory in an effort to understand myself and my situation. I was always trying new ways of coping with symptoms including my relentless auditory hallucinations. And perhaps most importantly of all, when I got out of bed in the morning, I always knew the reason why I had a purpose in life, I had been called, I had a vocation, and I kept saying yes to it. Even in the present I must make a daily affirmation of my vocation in order to keep going. The

temptation to give up is still strong sometimes.

My journey of recovery is still ongoing. I still struggle with symptoms, grieve the losses that I have sustained, and have had to get involved in treatment for the sequela child abuse. I am also involved in self help and mutual support and I still use professional services including medications, psychotherapy, and hospitals. However, now I do not just take medication or go to the hospital. I have learned to use medications and to use the hospital. This is the active stance that is the hallmark of the recovery process.

There is more to the recovery process than simply recovering from mental illness. We must also recovery from the effects of poverty and second class citizenship. We must learn to raise our consciousness and find our collective pride in order to overcome internalized stigma. Finally, many of us emerge from mental health treatment settings with traumatic stress disorders related to having sustained or witnessed physical, sexual and/or emotional abuse at the hands of staff. As one long term veteran of mental health services wrote:

> The stuff I've been through was like a nightmare. Sometimes I go back into the nightmare. I cry every night about it. Remembering it is like being in the nightmare again . . .Sometimes I scream at night because I dream about the hospital I was raped in or some other hospital I've been in (LaLime 1990).

Sometimes recovering from mental illness is the easy part. Recovering from these deep wounds to the human heart takes much longer.

Recovery does not mean cure. Rather recovery is an attitude, a stance, and a way of approaching the day's challenges. It is not a perfectly linear journey. There are times of rapid gains and disappointing relapses. There are times of just living, just staying quiet, resting and regrouping. Each person's journey of recovery is unique. Each person must find what works for them. This means that we must have the opportunity to try and to fail and to try again. In order to support the recovery process mental health professionals must not rob us of the opportunity to fail. Professionals must embrace the concept of the dignity of risk and the right to failure if they are to be supportive of us.

In closing, I would like to add that all around the world, people who have been psychiatrically labeled are organizing. We are organizing on the local, statewide, national, and international level. We are developing a collective voice and are fighting to overcome oppression, poverty, discrimination, and stigma. We are saying no to second class health care, poor or non existent housing, and to the indignities that so often come with psychiatric hospitalizations including the barbaric use of restraint and seclusion. We are sitting at the table in dialogue with service providers and policy makers to find alternatives to involuntary treatment. We are joining with other disability groups to form a broad coalition of 40 million Americans with disabilities to achieve equity in healthcare, support services, and entitlements.

We are also beginning to define our experiences in our own terms and to educate mental health professionals about our experience and what helps. We are fortunate to have the National Empowerment Center in Lawrence, Massachusetts. The National Empowerment Center is a completely consumer run and controlled national technical assistance center supported through funding from the Center for Mental Health Services. We have developed many innovative trainings and resources. For instance, we have a new training available that is entitled Hearing Voices That Are Distressing: A

> **"O**UR GREATEST CHALLENGE IS TO FIND A WAY TO REFUSE TO BE DEHUMANIZED IN THE AGE OF MANAGED PROFIT, AND TO BE BOLD AND BRAVE AND DARING ENOUGH TO REMAIN HUMAN HEARTED WHILE WORKING IN THE HUMAN SERVICES."

Simulated Training Experience and Self-help Strategies. In this workshop designed for mental health practitioners and students, participants listen to an audiotape that was designed by people who hear voices to simulate the experience of hearing voices that are distressing. Participants listen to the tape while having to undergo a series of tasks including a mental status exam, a community outing, a day treatment activity group, and psychological testing. After the simulated training participants have the opportunity to learn many self-help strategies that help to control or eliminate distressing voices.

A new age is upon us. We must help the students of today to understand that people with psychiatric disabilities are human beings with human hearts. Our

hearts are as real and as vulnerable and as valuable as yours are. Understanding that people with psychiatric disabilities are first and foremost people who are in process, growing and changing is the cornerstone of understanding the concept of recovery. We must not let our hearts grow hard and calloused toward people with psychiatric disabilities. Our role is not to judge who will and will not recover. Our job is to create environments in which opportunities for recovery and empowerment exist. Our job is to establish strong, supportive relationships with those we work with. And perhaps most of all, our greatest challenge is to find a way to refuse to be dehumanized in the age of managed profit, and to be bold and brave and daring enough to remain human hearted while working in the human services.

REFERENCES

LaLime, W. (1990). Untitled speech used as part of Lowell MPOWER's anti stigma workshop, Lowell Massachusetts.

Deegan, P. (1990). Spirit breaking: When the helping professions hurt. *The Humanistic Psychologist, 18*(3), 301-313.

Lefcourt, H. M. (1973). The function of the illusions of control and freedom. *American Psychologist, 28*, 417-425.

Seligman, M. E. P. (1975). *Helplessness: On depression, development and death.* San Francisco: Freeman.

Can J Diabetes 37 (2013) S20–S25

Contents lists available at SciVerse ScienceDirect

Canadian Journal of Diabetes

journal homepage:
www.canadianjournalofdiabetes.com

Clinical Practice Guidelines

Organization of Diabetes Care

Canadian Diabetes Association Clinical Practice Guidelines Expert Committee

The initial draft of this chapter was prepared by Maureen Clement MD, CCFP,
Betty Harvey RNEC, BScN, MScN, Doreen M. Rabi MD, MSc, FRCPC,
Robert S. Roscoe BScPharm, ACPR, CDE, Diana Sherifali RN, PhD, CDE

KEY MESSAGES

- Diabetes care should be organized around the person living with diabetes who is practising self-management and is supported by a proactive, interprofessional team with specific training in diabetes.
- Diabetes care should be delivered using as many elements as possible of the chronic care model.
- The following strategies have the best evidence for improved outcomes and should be used: promotion of self-management, including self-management support and education; interprofessional team-based care with expansion of professional roles, in cooperation with the collaborating physician, to include monitoring or medication adjustment and disease (case) management, including patient education, coaching, treatment adjustment, monitoring and care coordination.
- Diabetes care should be structured, evidence based and supported by a clinical information system that includes electronic patient registries, clinician and patient reminders, decision support, audits and feedback.

HELPFUL HINTS BOX: ORGANIZATION OF CARE

Recognize: Consider diabetes risk factors for all of your patients and screen appropriately for diabetes.

Register: Develop a registry for all of your patients with diabetes.

Resource: Support self-management through the use of interprofessional teams which could include the primary care provider, diabetes educator, dietitian, nurse, pharmacist and other specialists.

Relay: Facilitate information sharing between the person with diabetes and the team for coordinated care and timely management changes.

Recall: Develop a system to remind your patients and caregivers of timely review and reassessment.

Introduction

In Canada, there is a care gap between the clinical goals outlined in evidence-based guidelines for diabetes management and real-life clinical practice (1,2). Since almost 80% of the care of people with diabetes takes place in the primary care setting, there has been a shift toward delivering diabetes care in the primary care setting using the chronic care model (CCM) (3–5). The CCM is an organizational approach as well as a quality improvement (QI) strategy in caring for people with chronic diseases, the elements of which are evidence based. These elements facilitate planning and coordination among providers while helping patients play an informed role in managing their own care (6). Previous recommendations in this chapter, in 2008, focused on the daily commitment of the individual with diabetes to self-management, with the support of the interprofessional diabetes healthcare team. Although these are still critical elements of diabetes care, increasing evidence suggests that the CCM, which includes elements beyond the patient and healthcare provider, provides a framework for the optimal care of persons with diabetes (6–8). This chapter has been revised to reflect the importance of the CCM design, delivery and organization of diabetes care. Despite the use of new terminology (Table 1), many of the previous recommendations have remained the same but have been reorganized to fall under specific components of the CCM and broadened to include elements such as the health system and the community (9). This is intended to assist the readers in increasing their understanding and use of the CCM framework in their daily practice.

The CCM and Organization of Diabetes Care

In many ways, diabetes care has been the prototype for the CCM (Figure 1). Developed in the late 1990s, this model aims to transform the care of patients with chronic illnesses from acute and reactive to proactive, planned and population based. This model has been adopted by many countries as well as several provinces in Canada (13). Early studies showed that the following interventions improved care in the chronically ill: educating and supporting the patient, team-based care, increasing the healthcare provider's skills and use of registry-based information systems (7,8,10). The current CCM has expanded on this evidence to include the following 6 elements that work together to strengthen the provider-patient relationship and improve health outcomes: 1) delivery systems design, 2) self-management support, 3) decision support, 4) clinical information systems, 5) the community, and 6) health systems. A recent systematic review found that primary care practices were able to successfully implement the CCM (6). Furthermore, incorporating most or all of the CCM elements has been associated with improved quality of care and disease outcomes in patients with various chronic illnesses, including

1499-2671/$ – see front matter © 2013 Canadian Diabetes Association
http://dx.doi.org/10.1016/j.jcjd.2013.01.014

Table 1
Definition of terms (9–12)

Terminology	
Chronic care model (CCM)	The CCM is an organizational approach to caring for people with chronic diseases as well as a quality improvement strategy, the elements of which are evidence based. These elements facilitate planning and coordination among providers while helping patients play an informed role in managing their own care. This model has evolved from the original Wagner CCM (1999) to the expanded care model (9).
Elements of CCM	1) Delivery systems designs 2) Self-management support 3) Decision support 4) Clinical information 5) The community 6) Health systems
Primary care	First contact and ongoing healthcare: family physicians, general practitioners and nurse practitioners
Shared care	Joint participation of primary care physicians and specialty care physicians in the planned delivery of care, informed by an enhanced information exchange over and above routine discharge and referral notices Can also refer to the sharing of responsibility for care between the patient and provider or team
Quality Improvement Strategies	
Audit and feedback	Summary of provider or group performance on clinical or process indicators delivered to clinicians to increase awareness of performance
Clinical information systems	The part of an information system that helps organize patient and population data to facilitate efficient and effective care. May provide timely reminders for providers and patients, identify relevant subpopulations for proactive care, facilitate individual patient care planning, and share information with patients and providers to coordinate care or monitor performance of practice team and care system.
Clinician reminders	Paper-based or electronic system to prompt healthcare professionals to recall patient-specific information (e.g. A1C) or do a specific task (e.g. foot exam)
Collaboration	A collaborative intervention is a method used to help healthcare organizations apply continuous quality improvement techniques and affect organizational change.
Continuous quality improvement	Techniques for examining and measuring clinical processes, designing interventions, testing their impacts and then assessing the need for further improvement
Decision support	Integration of evidence-based guidelines into the flow of clinical practice
Disease (case) management	A structured, multifaceted intervention that supports the practitioner/patient relationship and plan of care; emphasizes prevention of exacerbations and complications utilizing evidence-based practice guidelines and patient empowerment strategies May include education, coaching, treatment adjustment, monitoring and care coordination, often by a nurse, pharmacist or dietitian
Facilitated relay of information to clinician	Clinical information collected from patients and sent to clinicians, other than the existing medical record (e.g. pharmacist sending SMBG results)
Patient registry	A list of patients sharing a common characteristic, such as a diabetes registry May be paper based but increasingly is electronic, ranging from a simple spreadsheet to one embedded in an electronic health record
Patient reminders	Any effort to remind patients about upcoming appointments or aspects of self-care (e.g. glucose monitoring)
Self-management education (SME)	A systematic intervention that involves active patient participation in self-monitoring (physiological processes) and/or decision making (managing) (see Self-Management Education chapter, p. S26)
Self-management support	In addition to SME strategies that enhance patients' ability to manage their condition, including internal and community resources, such as disease management with patient reminders, monitoring and linage to self-management support/interest groups
Team changes	Changes to the structure of a primary healthcare team, such as: • Adding a team member or shared care, such as a physician, nurse specialist or pharmacist • Using an interdisciplinary team in primary routine management • Expansion of professional role (e.g. nurse or pharmacist has a more active role in monitoring or adjusting medications)
Other Terms	
Lay leader	Trained and accredited non-healthcare professional delivering a program that adopts a philosophy of self-management rather than the medical model
Telehealth	Delivery of health-related services and information via telecommunications technology

A1C, glycated hemoglobin; *SMBG*, self-monitoring of blood glucose.

diabetes (6,8,10,14–16). A recent systematic review and meta-analysis of QI strategies on the management of diabetes concluded that interventions targeting the system of chronic disease management along with patient-mediated QI strategies should be an important component of interventions aimed at improving care. Although some of the improvements were modest, it may be that, when the QI components are used together, there is a synergistic effect as noted in the above studies (12).

CCM in Diabetes

Initial analyses of CCM interventions for improving diabetes care suggested that a multifaceted intervention was the key to QI

(8,15,17). Organizations that provided diabetes care in accordance with the CCM provided better quality care than did organizations that were less likely to use elements of this model (18). Furthermore, the degree to which care delivered in a primary care setting conforms to the CCM has been shown to be an important predictor of the 10-year risk of coronary heart disease (CHD) in patients with type 2 diabetes (19). Initially, it appeared as if only process outcomes, such as behaviours of patients and caregivers, are improved with the CCM; however, with longer-term use of the model in clinical practice, improvements in clinical outcomes also are noted, such as reductions in glycated hemoglobin (A1C) and low-density lipoprotein cholesterol (LDL-C) levels (20). A large, 2-arm, cluster-randomized, QI trial, using all 6 dimensions of the

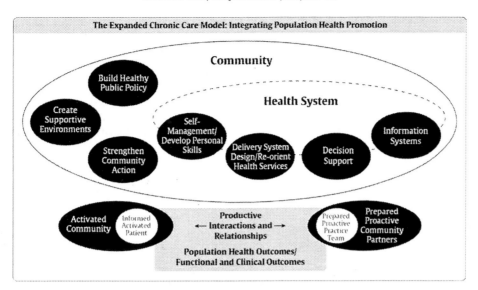

Figure 1. The Expanded Chronic Care Model: Integrating Population Health Promotion.
Used with permission from Barr VJ, Robinson S, Marin-Link B, et al. The expanded chronic care model: an integration of concepts and strategies from population health promotion and the chronic care model. Hosp Q. 2003;7:73–80.

CCM, found significant improvements in A1C and LDL-C and an increase in the use of statins and antiplatelet therapy among patients with diabetes (5). A recent meta-analysis of randomized controlled trials (RCTs) assessing the effectiveness of disease management programs for improving glycemic control found significant reductions in A1C with programs that included the fundamental elements of the CCM (21). Other trials found that use of the CCM improved cardiovascular (CV) risk factors in patients with diabetes (19,22). One large-scale analysis of a nationwide disease management program using the CCM and based in primary care reduced overall mortality as well as drug and hospital costs (23). The Assessment of Chronic Illness Care (ACIC) is a practical assessment as well as a research tool. It can help teams strategically involve themselves in a structured way to assess and identify gaps to develop into a more robust CCM (11).

Elements of the CCM that Improve Care

Delivery systems design

The team

Current evidence continues to support the importance of a multi- and interprofessional team with specific training in diabetes within the primary care setting (10,12,21). The team should work collaboratively with the primary care provider who, in turn, should be supported by a diabetes specialist. Specialist support may be direct or indirect through shared care, an interdisciplinary team member or educational support (5,12). In adults with type 2 diabetes, this care model has been associated with improvements in A1C, blood pressure (BP), lipids and care processes compared to care that is delivered by a specialist or primary care physician alone (5,24–27). A reduction in preventable, diabetes-related emergency room visits also has been noted when the team includes a specifically trained nurse who follows detailed treatment algorithms for diabetes care (25). In Canada, observational data from primary care networks, whose approach is to improve access and coordinate care, suggest that patients who are part of these interdisciplinary teams have better outcomes and fewer hospital visits than patients who are not (28).

Team membership may be extensive and should include various disciplines. Those disciplines associated with improved diabetes outcomes include nurses, nurse practitioners, dietitians, pharmacists and providers of psychological support.

Nurses have always been, and continue to be, core members of the team. A systematic review (26) and recent meta-analysis (29) found that case management led by specialist nurses or dietitians improved both glycemic control and CV risk factors. Another study found improved BP outcomes with nurse-led interventions vs. usual care, particularly when nurses followed algorithms and were able to prescribe (30). In addition, a large RCT found that nurse-led, guideline-based, collaborative care management was associated with improvements in A1C, lipids, BP and depression in patients with depression and type 2 diabetes and/or CHD (31). Practices with nurse practitioners also were found to have better diabetes process outcomes than those with physicians alone or those employing only physician assistants (32). Small-group or individualized nutrition counselling by a registered dietitian with expertise in diabetes management is another important element of team-based care. A variety of individual and community health-care support systems, particularly psychological support, can also improve glycemic control (33).

Recent meta-analyses involving people with both type 1 and type 2 diabetes showed a significant 0.76% drop in A1C (34) as well as improved adherence and quality of life (QOL) and reductions in adverse drug reactions and LDL-C with collaborative pharmacist intervention (35). A Canadian randomized trial that added a pharmacist to primary care teams showed a significant reduction in BP for people with type 2 diabetes (36). Therefore, pharmacists can play a key role in diabetes management, beyond that of dispensing medications.

Roles within the team and disease management

Flexibility in the operation of the team is important. Team changes, such as adding a team member, active participation of professionals from more than one discipline and role expansion, have been associated with improved clinical outcomes (10,12,21). The greatest body of evidence for improved clinical outcomes in diabetes is with promotion of self-management, team changes and case or disease management programs (5,10,12,21,27,37,38). In a systematic review and meta-analysis of QI strategies, the following QI strategy improved clinical outcomes, such as A1C, BP and cholesterol, as well as process outcomes, medication use and screening for complications: promotion of self-management, team changes, case management, patient education, facilitated relay, electronic patient registries, patient reminders, audits and feedback, and clinician reminders. The effectiveness of different QI strategies may vary based on the baseline A1C, with QI targeting professionals only beneficial when the baseline A1C control is poor. In practice, many of these QI strategies occur in concert with one another through the use of interprofessional teams.

Another recent meta-analysis by Pimouguet et al. (21) defines disease management as the "ongoing and proactive follow-up of patients that includes at least 2 of the following 5 components: patient education, coaching, treatment adjustment (where the manager is able to start or modify treatment with or without prior approval from the primary care physician), monitoring, care coordination (where the manager reminds the patient about upcoming appointments or important aspects of self-care and informs the physician about complications, treatment adjustments, or therapeutic recommendations)." The meta-analysis found that a high frequency of patient contact and the ability of the disease manager to start or modify treatment with or without prior approval from the primary care physician had the greatest impact on A1C lowering. Disease management programs also were more effective for patients with poor glycemic control (A1C ≥8%) at baseline (21). Other disease management strategies that have been associated with positive outcomes are the delegation of prescription authority and the monitoring of complications using decision support tools (26,27,30).

The primary care provider, who is usually a family physician, has a unique role in the team, particularly with regard to providing continuity of care. He or she is often the principal medical contact for the person with diabetes and has a comprehensive understanding of all health issues and social supports (39). In the past, there was some debate over whether specialist care or primary care yields better diabetes outcomes (40–43). Although physicians practising in hospital-based diabetes centres may be more likely to adhere to guidelines (44), general practice-based care is associated with higher patient follow-up (45). Certainly, there are patients with diabetes who may require ongoing, specialized care, such as children and pregnant women. There is also evidence that specialized care may be more beneficial in people with type 1 diabetes (46,47). In the CCM, collaborative, shared care is the ideal. However, the results of one Cochrane review did not support shared care (48). It should be noted, however, that several of the studies included in this analysis did not use all the elements of the CCM. Other, more recent studies have supported the shared care model (49) and have shown that specialist input into specialized diabetes teams at the interface of primary and secondary care improves care (5,50).

Self-management support

Self-management support, including self-management education, is the cornerstone of diabetes care in the CCM. Self-management education goes well beyond didactic disease-specific information. It is a systematic intervention that involves active patient participation in self-monitoring (physiological processes) and/or decision making (managing). Self-management enables the person with diabetes to take an active role in managing his or her own care through problem solving and goal setting, which can be facilitated through the use of motivational interviewing techniques. Self-management support, often through disease or case management, with strategies such as patient reminders, helps the individual in self-management. Evidence for diabetes self-management support and education is robust (12) and is covered in more detail in the next chapter (see Self-Management Education chapter, p. S26).

Decision support

Providing healthcare practitioners with best practice information at the point of care to help support decision making has been shown to improve outcomes. In a systematic review, evidence-based guideline interventions, particularly those that used interactive computer technology to provide recommendations and immediate feedback of personally tailored information, were the most effective in improving patient outcomes (51). A randomized trial using electronic medical record (EMR) decision support in primary care found improvement in A1C (52), and a cluster randomized trial of a QI program found that the provision of a clear treatment protocol—supported by tailored postgraduate education of the primary care physician and case coaching by an endocrinologist—substantially improved the overall quality of diabetes care provided, as well as major diabetes-related outcomes (50). Incorporation of evidence-based treatment algorithms has been shown in several studies to be an integral part of diabetes case management (10,26,30,31). Even the use of simple decision support tools, such as clinical flow sheets, have been associated with improved adherence to clinical practice guidelines for diabetes (53).

Clinical information systems

Clinical information systems (CIS) that allow for a population-based approach to diabetes assessment and management, such as EMRs or electronic patient registries, have been shown to have a positive impact on evidence-based diabetes care (10,12,54,55). Practice-level clinical registries give an overview of an entire practice, which may assist in the delivery and monitoring of patient care. In addition to providing clinical information at the time of a patient encounter, CIS also can help promote timely management and reduce the tendency toward clinical inertia (56). Provincial- and national-level registries are also essential for benchmarking, tracking diabetes trends, determining the effect of QI programs, and for resource planning.

Other quality improvement strategies

Audits and feedback generally lead to small but potentially important improvements in professional practice and seem to depend on baseline performance and how the feedback is provided (57). Facilitated relay of information to clinicians may include electronic or web-based methods through which patients provide self-care data and the clinician reviews have been shown to improve care. Ideally, this should occur in case management with a team member who has prescribing or ordering ability (12). Physician and patient reminders also have shown benefit (12,50).

Community

Environmental factors, such as food security, the ability to lead an active lifestyle, as well as access to care and social supports, also impact diabetes outcomes. Although community resources have not traditionally been integrated into care, community partnerships should be considered as a means of obtaining better care for patients with diabetes. For example, in addition to the diabetes health team, peer- or lay leader-led self-management groups have been shown to be beneficial in persons with type 2 diabetes (58,59).

Health systems

Support for diabetes care from the broader level of the healthcare system, such as the national and provincial systems, is essential. A number of provinces have adopted an expanded CCM (9) that includes health promotion and disease prevention (13). Many provinces and health regions also have developed diabetes strategies, diabetes service frameworks and support diabetes collaboratives. Some trials on diabetes-specific collaboratives have been shown to improve clinical outcomes (22,50,60), although a recent meta-analysis on continuous QI failed to show benefit (12).

Provider incentives represent another area of health system support. Some provinces have added incentive billing codes for patients with diabetes so that providers can be financially compensated for the use of flow sheets as well as time spent collaborating with the patient for disease planning (61). Pay-for-performance programs, which encourage the achievement of goals through reimbursement, are more commonly used outside of Canada. To date, these programs have had mixed results (62–64). Various payment systems also have been studied, but it is still unclear which of these may improve diabetes outcomes (65,66). Incentives to physicians to enroll patients and provide care within a nation-wide disease management program appears to be effective (23), as does infrastructure incentive payments that encourage the CCM (16). A meta-analysis that included physician incentives as a QI has shown mixed results for improved outcomes (12).

Telehealth

Although not a specific element of the CCM, telehealth technologies may help facilitate many components of this model. These technologies may be used for conferencing or education of team members; telemonitoring of health data, such as glucose readings

or BP; disease management via telephone or internet; or tele-consultation with specialists. Telehealth also appears to be effective for diabetes self-management education and has been associated with improvements in metabolic control and reductions in CV risk (67). One RCT and 2 systematic reviews of telemonitoring of various disease management parameters, ranging from blood glucose results to foot temperature, found improved outcomes with tele-monitoring, such as A1C lowering, a lower incidence of foot ulcerations and better QOL (4,68,69). These benefits were noted regardless of whether the teleconsultation was asynchronous or synchronous (69).

RECOMMENDATIONS

1. Diabetes care should be proactive, incorporate elements of the chronic care model (CCM), and be organized around the person living with diabetes who is supported in self-management by an interprofessional team with specific training in diabetes [Grade C, Level 3 (6,23)].

2. The following quality improvement strategies should be used, alone or in combination, to improve glycemic control [Grade A, Level 1 (12)]:
   a) Promotion of self-management
   b) Team changes
   c) Disease (case) management
   d) Patient education
   e) Facilitated relay of clinical information
   f) Electronic patient registries
   g) Patient reminders
   h) Audit and feedback
   i) Clinician education
   j) Clinician reminders (with or without decision support)

3. Diabetes care management by an interprofessional team with specific training in diabetes and supported by specialist input should be integrated within diabetes care delivery models in the primary care [Grade A, Level 1A (12,21)] and specialist care [Grade D, Consensus] settings.

4. The role of the diabetes case manager should be enhanced, in cooperation with the collaborating physician [Grade A, Level 1A (12,21)], including interventions led by a nurse [Grade A, Level 1A (29,30)], pharmacist [Grade B, Level 2 (34)] or dietitian [Grade B, Level 2 (70)], to improve coordination of care and facilitate timely diabetes management changes.

5. As part of a collaborative, shared care approach within the CCM, an interprofessional team with specialized training in diabetes, and including a physician diabetes expert, should be used in the following groups:
   a) Children with diabetes [Grade D, Level 4 (71)]
   b) Type 1 diabetes [Grade C, Level 3 (46)]
   c) Women with diabetes who require preconception counselling [Grade C, Level 3 (72–74)] and women with diabetes in pregnancy [Grade D, Consensus]
   d) Individuals with complex (multiple diabetes-related complications) type 2 diabetes who are not reaching targets [Grade D, Consensus]

6. Telehealth technologies may be used as part of a disease management program to:
   1. Improve self-management in underserviced communities [Grade B, Level 2 (67)]
   2. Facilitate consultation with specialized teams as part of a shared-care model [Grade A, Level 1A (69)]

Abbreviation:
CCM, chronic care model.

Other Relevant Guidelines

Self-Management Education, p. S26
Type 1 Diabetes in Children and Adolescents, p. S153
Type 2 Diabetes in Children and Adolescents, p. S163
Diabetes and Pregnancy, p. S168

Relevant Appendix

Appendix 2. Sample Diabetes Patient Care Flow Sheet for Adults

References

1. Harris SB, Ekoé J-M, Zdanowicz Y, et al. Glycemic control and morbidity in the Canadian primary care setting (results of the Diabetes in Canada Evaluation Study). Diabetes Res Clin Pract 2005;70:90–7.
2. Braga M, Casanova A, Teoh H, et al. Treatment gaps in the management of cardiovascular risk factors in patients with type 2 diabetes in Canada. Can J Cardiol 2010;26:297–302.
3. Jaakkimainen L, Shah B, Kopp A. Sources of physician care for people with diabetes. In: Hux J, Booth G, Slaughter P, et al., editors. Diabetes in Ontario: An ICES Practice Atlas, 6. Toronto, ON: Institute for Clinical Evaluative Sciences; 2003. p. 161–92.
4. Jaana M, Pare G. Home telemonitoring of patients with diabetes: a systematic assessment of observed effects. J Eval Clin Pract 2007;13:242–53.
5. Borgermans L, Goderis G, Van Den Broeke C, et al. Interdisciplinary diabetes care teams operating on the interface between primary and specialty care are associated with improved outcomes of care: findings from the Leuven Diabetes Project. BMC Health Serv Res 2009;9:179.
6. Coleman K, Austin B, Brach C, Wagner EH. Evidence on the chronic care model in the new millennium. Health Affairs 2009;28:75–85.
7. Wagner EH, Austin BT, Von Korff M. Organizing care for patients with chronic illness. Milbank Q 1996;74:511–44.
8. Renders CM, Valk GD, Griffin S, et al. Interventions to improve the management of diabetes mellitus in primary care, outpatient, and community settings. Cochrane Database Syst Rev 2001;1:CD001481.
9. Barr VJ, Robinson S, Marin-Link B, Underhill L, et al. The expanded chronic care model: an integration of concepts and strategies from population health promotion and the chronic care model. Hosp Q 2003;7:73–80.
10. Shojania KG, Ranjii SR, McDonald KM, et al. Effects of quality improvement strategies for type 2 diabetes on glycemic control: a meta-regression analysis. JAMA 2006;296:427–40.
11. Improving Chronic Illness Care. Available at: http://www.improvingchroniccare.org/index.php?p=ACIC_Survey&s=35. Accessed February 24, 2013.
12. Tricco AC, Ivers NM, Grimshaw JM, et al. Effectiveness of quality improvement strategies on the management of diabetes: a systematic review and meta-analysis. Lancet; 2012:12–21.
13. Health Canada Council. Progress Report 2011: Health care renewal in Canada. May 2011. Available at: http://www.healthcouncilcanada.ca/tree/2.45-2011Progress_ENG.pdf. Accessed February 24, 2013.
14. Minkman M, Kees A, Robbert H. Performance improvement based on integrated quality management models: what evidence do we have? A systematic literature review. Int J Qual Health Care 2007;19:90–104.
15. Piatt GA, Orchard TJ, Emerson S, et al. Translating the chronic care model into the community. Diabetes Care 2006;29:811–7.
16. Gabbay RA, Bailit MH, Mauger DT, et al. Multipayer patient-centered medical home implementation guided by the chronic care model. Jt Comm J Qual Patient Saf 2011;37:265–73.
17. Bodenheimer T, Wagner EH, Grumbach K. Improving primary care for patients with chronic illness: the chronic care model, part 2. JAMA 2002;288:1909–14.
18. Fleming B, Silver A, Ocepek-Welikson K, et al. The relationship between organizational systems and clinical quality in diabetes care. Am J Manag Care 2004;10:934–44.

19. Parchman ML, Zeber JE, Romero RR, et al. Risk of coronary artery disease in type 2 diabetes and the delivery of care consistent with the chronic care model in primary care settings: a STARNet study. Med Care 2007;45:1129–34.

20. Chin MH, Drum ML, Guillen M, et al. Improving and sustaining diabetes care in community health centers with the health disparities collaboratives. Med Care 2007;45:1135–43.

21. Pimouguet C, Le GM, Thiebaut R, et al. Effectiveness of disease-management programs for improving diabetes care: a meta-analysis. CMAJ 2011;183: e115–27.

22. Vargas RB, Mangione CM, Asch S, et al. Can a chronic care model collaborative reduce heart disease risk in patients with diabetes. J Gen Intern Med 2007;22: 215–22.

23. Stock S, Drabik A, Buscher G, et al. German diabetes management programs improve quality of care and curb costs. Health Affairs 2010;29:2197–205.

24. vanBruggen R, Gorter K, Stolk R, et al. Clinical inertia in general practice: widespread and related to the outcome of diabetes care. Fam Pract 2009;26: 428–36.

25. Davidson MB, Blanco-Castellanos M, Duran P. Integrating nurse-directed diabetes management into a primary care setting. Am J Manag Care 2010;16: 652–6.

26. Saxena S, Misra T, Car J, et al. Systematic review of primary healthcare interventions to improve diabetes outcomes in minority ethnic groups. J Ambul Care Manage 2007;30:218–30.

27. Willens D, Cripps R, Wilson A, et al. Interdisciplinary team care for diabetic patients by primary care physicians, advanced practice nurses and clinical Pharmacists. Clin Diabetes 2011;29:60–8.

28. Manns BJ, Tonelli M, Zhang J, et al. Enrolment in primary care networks: impact on outcomes and processes of care for patients with diabetes. CMAJ 2012;184: e144–52.

29. Welch G, Garb J, Zagarins S, et al. Nurse diabetes case management interventions and blood glucose control: results of a meta-analysis. Diabetes Res Clin Pract 2010;88:1–6.

30. Clark CE, Smith LFP, Taylor RS, et al. Nurse-led interventions used to improve control of high blood pressure in people with diabetes: a systematic review and meta-analysis. Diabet Med 2011;28:250–61.

31. Katon WJ. Collaborative care for patients with depression and chronic disease. N Engl J Med 2010;363:2611–20.

32. Ohman-Strickland PA, Orzano AJ, Hudson SV, et al. Quality of diabetes care in family medicine practices: influence of nurse-practitioners and physician's assistants. Ann Fam Med 2008;6:14–22.

33. Ismail K, Winkley K, Rabe-Hesketh S. Systemic review and meta-analysis of randomized controlled trial of psychological interventions to improve glycaemic control in patients with type 2 diabetes. Lancet 2004;363:1589–97.

34. Collins C, Limone BL, Scholle JM, et al. Effect of pharmacist interventions on glycemic control in diabetes. Diabetes Res Clin Pract 2011;92:145–52.

35. Chisholm-Burns MA, Kim Lee J, Spivey CA, et al. U.S. pharmacists' effect as team members on patient care: systematic review and meta-analyses. Med Care 2010;48:923–33.

36. Simpson SH, Majumdar SR, Tsuyuki RT, et al. Effect of adding pharmacists to primary care teams on blood pressure control in patients with type 2 diabetes: a randomized controlled trial (ISRCTN97121854). Diabetes Care. Available at: http://care.diabetesjournals.org/content/early/2010/10/05/dc10-1294.full.pdf+html; 2010. Accessed February 24, 2013.

37. vanBruggen JAR, Gorter K, Stolk R. Shared and delegated systems are not quick remedies for improving diabetes care: a systematic review. Prim Care Diabetes 2007;1:59–68.

38. Cleveringa FGW, Gorter KJ, Van Donk MD, et al. Combined task delegation, computerized decision support, and feedback improve cardiovascular risk for type 2 diabetic patients. Diabetes Care 2008;31:2273–5.

39. Cabana MD, Jee SH. Does continuity of care improve patient outcomes? J Fam Pract 2004;53:974–80.

40. Aron D, Pogach L. Specialists versus generalists in the era of pay for performance: "a plague o' both your houses!". Qual Saf Health Care 2007;16:3–5.

41. McAlister FA, Majumdar SR, Eurich DT, et al. The effect of specialist care within the first year on subsequent outcomes in 24 232 adults with new onset diabetes mellitus: population-based cohort study. Qual Saf Health Care 2007; 16:6–11.

42. Shah BR, Hux JE, Laupacis A, et al. Diabetic patients with a prior specialist care have better glycaemic control than those with prior primary care. J Eval Clin Pract 2005;11:568–75.

43. Post PN, Wittenberg J, Burgers JS. Do specialized centers and specialist produce better outcomes for patients with chronic disease than primary care generalists? A systematic review. Int J Qual Health Care 2009;21:387–96.

44. Gnavi R, Picariello R, Karaghiosoff L, et al. Determinants of quality in diabetes care process: the population-based Torino study. Diabetes Care 2009;32: 1986–92.

45. Griffin SJ, Kimonth AL. WITHDRAWN: Systems for routine surveillance in people with diabetes mellitus. Cochrane Database Syst Rev 2009;1:CD000541.

46. Zgibor JC, Songer TJ, Kelsey SF, et al. Influence of health care providers on the development of diabetes complications: long term follow-up from the Pittsburgh Epidemiology of Diabetes Complications Study. Diabetes Care 2002;25: 1584–90.

47. Tabak A, Tamas G, Zgibor J. Targets and reality: a comparison of health care indicators in the U.S. (Pittsburgh Epidemiology of Diabetes Complications Study) and Hungary (Diab Care Hungary). Diabetes Care 2000;23:1284–9.

48. Smith SM, Allwright S, O'Dowd T. Effectiveness of shared care across the interface between primary and specialty care in chronic disease management. Cochrane Database Syst Rev 2007;3:CD004910.

49. Cheung N, Yue D, Kotowitz MA, et al. Care delivery: a comparison of diabetes clinics with different emphasis on routine care, complications assessment and shared care. Diabet Med 2008;25:974–8.

50. Goderis G, Borgermans L, Grol R, et al. Start improving the quality of care for people with type 2 diabetes through a general practice support program: a cluster randomized trial. Diabetes Res Clin Pract 2010;88:56–64.

51. de Belvis A, Pelone F, Biasco A, et al. Can primary care professionals' adherence to evidence based medicine tools improve quality of care in type 2 diabetes? A systematic review. Diabetes Res Clin Pract 2009;85:119–31.

52. O'Connor PJ, Sperl-Hillen JM, Rush WA, et al. Impact of electronic health record clinical decision support on diabetes care: a randomized trial. Ann Fam Med 2011;9:12–21.

53. Hahn K, Ferrante C, Crosson J, et al. Diabetes flow sheet use associated with guideline adherence. Ann Fam Med 2008;6:235–8.

54. Grant RW, Hamrick HE, Sullivan CM, et al. Impact of population management with direct physician feedback on care of patients with type 2 diabetes. Diabetes Care 2003;26:2275–80.

55. Boren S, Puchbauer A, Williams F. Computerized prompting and feedback of diabetes care: a review of the literature. J Diabetes Sci Technol 2009;3:944–50.

56. Sperl-Hillen J, Averbeck B, Palattao K, et al. Outpatient EHR-based diabetes clinical decision support that works: lessons learned from implementing diabetes wizard. Diabetes Spectrum 2010;23:2010.

57. Ivers N, Jamtvedt G, Flottorp S, et al. Audit and feedback: effects on professional practice and healthcare outcomes. Cochrane Database Syst Rev 2012;6: CD000259.

58. Deakin T, McShane CE, Cade JE, et al. Group based training for self-management strategies in people with type 2 diabetes mellitus. Cochrane Database Syst Rev 2005;2:CD003417.

59. Foster G, Taylor SJ, Eldridge SE, et al. Self-management education programmes by lay leaders for people with chronic conditions. Cochrane Database Syst Rev 2007;4:CD005108.

60. Schouten LM, Hulscher ME, van Everdingen JJ, et al. Evidence for the impact of quality improvement collaboratives: systematic review. BMJ 2008;336: 1491–4.

61. Canadian Diabetes Association. Type of incentive billings by province. Available at: www.diabetes.ca/documents/for-professionals/Billing-Chart-Final.pdf. Accessed February 24, 2013.

62. Chen TT, Chung KP, Lin IC, et al. The unintended consequence of diabetes mellitus pay-for-performance (P4P) program in Taiwan: are patients with more comorbidities or more severe conditions likely to be excluded from the P4P program? Health Serv Res 2011;46:47–60.

63. Mannion R, Davies H. Payment for performance in health care. BMJ 2008;336: 306–8.

64. Dalton AR, Alshamsan R, Majeed A, Millett C. Exclusion of patients from quality measurement of diabetes care in the UK pay-for-performance programme. Diabet Med 2011;28:525–31.

65. Tu K, Cauch-Dudek K, Chen Z. Comparison of primary care physician payment models in the management of hypertension. Can Fam Physician 2009;55: 719–27.

66. Yan C, Kingston-Riechers J, Chuck A. Institute of Health Economics (IHE) report: financial incentives to physician practices. A literature review of evaluations of physician remuneration models. Alberta, Canada: IHE; March 2009.

67. Davis RM, Hitch AD, Salaam MM. TeleHealth improves diabetes self-management in an underserved community: Diabetes TeleCare. Diabetes Care 2010;33:1712–7.

68. Stone RA, Rao RH, Sevick MA. Active care management supported by home telemonitoring in veterans with type 2 diabetes: The DiaTel randomized controlled trial. Diabetes Care 2010;33:478–84.

69. Verhoeven F, Tanja-Dijkstra K, Nijland N, et al. Asynchronous and synchronous teleconsultation for diabetes care: a systematic literature review. J Diabetes Sci Technol 2010;4:666–84.

70. Wolf AM, Conaway MR, Crowther JQ, et al. Translating lifestyle intervention to practice in obese patients with type 2 diabetes: Improving Control with Activity and Nutrition (ICAN) study. Diabetes Care 2004;27:1570–6.

71. Glasgow AM, Weissberg-Benchall J, Tynan WD, et al. Readmissions of children with diabetes mellitus to a children's hospital. Pediatrics 1991;88: 98–104.

72. Ray JG, O'Brien TE, Chan WS. Preconception care and the risk of congenital anomalies in the offspring of women with diabetes mellitus: a meta-analysis. QJM 2001;94:435–44.

73. Kitzmiller JL, Gavin LA, Gin GD, et al. Preconception care of diabetes. Glycemic control prevents congenital anomalies. JAMA 1991;265:731–6.

74. McElvy SS, Miodovnik M, Rosenn B, et al. A focused preconceptional and early pregnancy program in women with type 1 diabetes reduces perinatal mortality and malformation rates to general population levels. J Matern Fetal Med 2000; 9:14–20.

Can J Diabetes 37 (2013) S26–S30

Contents lists available at SciVerse ScienceDirect

Canadian Journal of Diabetes

journal homepage:
www.canadianjournalofdiabetes.com

Clinical Practice Guidelines

Self-Management Education

Canadian Diabetes Association Clinical Practice Guidelines Expert Committee

The initial draft of this chapter was prepared by Helen Jones RN, MSN, CDE, Lori D. Berard RN, CDE, Gail MacNeill BNSc, RN, MEd, CDE, Dana Whitham RD, MS, CDE, Catherine Yu MD, FRCPC, MHSc

KEY MESSAGES

- Offer collaborative and interactive self-management education (SME) interventions as they are more effective than didactic SME.
- Incorporate problem-solving skills for ongoing self-management of medical, social and emotional aspects of care into the traditional knowledge and technical skills content of educational interventions.
- Design patient-centred learning to empower individuals to make informed decisions toward achievement of patient-chosen goals.
- Individualize SME interventions according to type of diabetes and recommended therapy, the patient's ability and motivation for learning and change, and his or her culture and literacy level.
- Provide ongoing SME and comprehensive healthcare collaboratively to make SME most effective.

Introduction

Self-management education (SME) is defined as a systematic intervention that involves active patient participation in self-monitoring (physiological processes) and/or decision making (managing) (1). It recognizes that patient-provider collaboration and the enablement of problem-solving skills are crucial to the individual's ability for sustained self-care (2).

Several meta-analyses have demonstrated that SME is associated with clinically important benefits in persons with type 2 diabetes, such as reductions in glycated hemoglobin (A1C) of 0.36% to 0.81% (1,3,4). Improved quality of life (QOL) for persons with either type 1 or type 2 diabetes also has been demonstrated (5), as have other important self-care outcomes in those with type 2 diabetes, such as sustained weight loss and cardiovascular (CV) fitness for up to 4 years (6). One systematic review involving both type 1 and type 2 diabetes found that, as measures progressed from immediate to long-term outcomes, percentage of improved outcomes reduced (immediate learning 78.6%, intermediate behaviour change 50.0%, long-term clinical improvement 38.5%) (7). A 5-year follow-up of a patient-centred type 2 diabetes SME program resulted in no worsening of A1C, whereas the A1C in the control group rose 1.3% over the 5 years (8).

Diabetes SME is evolving from a traditional didactic teaching program to one using a variety of educational, psychological and behavioural interventions, and a combination of didactic, interactive and collaborative teaching methods that are tailored to the individual's specific needs (9). The content and skill-training components of SME must be individualized according to the type of diabetes and recommended therapy, the patient's ability, barriers, motivation for learning and change, culture and literacy level, and available resources (4,10,11). Models for systematizing, organizing and/or guiding the development of SME programs (12,13) share a 5-step problem-solving process aligned with the empowerment protocol (14) based on the principle that adults are more likely to make and maintain behaviour changes if these changes are personally meaningful and freely chosen (14). In order to meet the definition of "self-management education," problem-solving skills for ongoing self-management of medical, social and emotional aspects of care must be integrated into the traditional knowledge and technical skills content of educational interventions (2). These skills are needed to inform decisions and increase the individual's capacity and confidence to apply these skills in daily life situations (2). SME refers to any of the educational processes that provide persons with the knowledge, skills and motivation required to inform decisions and increase the individual's capacity and confidence to apply these skills in daily life situations. Self-management support (addressed in the Organization of Care chapter, p. S20) refers to policies and people that may support continuation of self-management behaviours across the lifespan but that are not specific to educational processes.

Self-identification of a problem or need for self-care behaviour by the individual is crucial to all cognitive-behavioural interventions (14,15). The healthcare provider's role is to collaboratively facilitate this awareness process (2). Standardized instruments, such as the Problem Areas in Diabetes (PAID) (16), Self-care Inventory-Revised (SCI-R 2005) (17) or Summary of Diabetes Self-Care Activities (18), may have value in this process (19), although they have been used mainly for research purposes.

Interventions targeting knowledge and skills

Basic knowledge and skill areas that are essential for SME are monitoring of relevant health parameters, healthy eating, physical activity, pharmacotherapy, prevention and management of hypo-/hyperglycemia, and prevention and surveillance of complications. Skill training should include using self-monitoring of blood glucose (SMBG), making appropriate dietary choices, incorporating an exercise regimen, using medications as recommended and adjusting medication (20,21).

1499-2671/$ – see front matter © 2013 Canadian Diabetes Association
http://dx.doi.org/10.1016/j.jcjd.2013.01.015

In general, education sessions provided to patients with diabetes have resulted in positive changes in diabetes-related knowledge (22), as well as psychological (23–26) and behavioural (23,27) domains. With respect to A1C, most trials involving group-based education have shown sustained A1C reductions (i.e. between 4 and 12 months), ranging from 0.4% to 0.7% (22,23,26,28). The Diabetes Education and Self-Management for Ongoing and Newly Diagnosed (DESMOND) trial, a structured group education program for persons with newly diagnosed type 2 diabetes, resulted in greater improvements in weight loss, smoking cessation and positive improvements in illness beliefs up to 12 months after diagnosis; however, no significant effect on A1C was noted at 12-month follow-up (25).

In those studies that used print-based education, significant changes in behaviours related to physical activity (27), stage-of-change progression (29), weight loss (27) and improvements in glucose control (30) have been noted. Randomized trials of computer- or video-based education models have demonstrated improvements in at least 1 behaviour change related to healthy eating and physical activity (7,31).

All trials evaluating a culturally appropriate education module (which incorporated cultural or religious beliefs, were offered in the patient's native language, adapted dietary advice to reflect cultural traditions and the patient's needs, and/or involved family members) have noted improvements in diabetes-related knowledge, self-management behaviours and clinical outcomes, with A1C reductions ranging from 0.5% to 1.8% (32–35). These findings demonstrate the importance of creating culturally relevant educational materials.

Interventions for content and materials geared toward patients with low literacy and numeracy can be successful in improving outcomes, such as A1C, self-efficacy and blood pressure (BP) (36). Training healthcare professionals in specific communication skills to address low literacy can also be effective (37,38).

While the majority of randomized controlled trials (RCTs) examining skill-training interventions used face-to-face individual sessions (39–43), some have used face-to-face group sessions (44), a combination of face-to-face group and individual sessions (26) and video-based programs for home viewing (45). One study that compared insulin-initiation skills training provided in a group vs. an individual setting found no difference in A1C, rate of hypoglycemia, BP, lipid profile or QOL between the 2 approaches; however, differences in weight gain and time spent in follow-up appointments or calls favoured individual training sessions (44). Most interventions were delivered by nurses (26,39,43,44) or diabetes educators (42). In general, skill-training interventions demonstrated positive changes or no significant differences in outcomes compared to control. For example, contrasting results were found in the 2 trials examining the impact of SMBG skills training: 1 study found an improvement in A1C, low-density lipoprotein cholesterol (LDL-C), body mass index (BMI) and self-care activities with skills training (40), whereas the other found no difference in A1C and BMI but an improvement in total cholesterol (TC) and TC to high-density lipoprotein cholesterol (HDL-C) ratio (41).

Cognitive-behavioural interventions

The acquisition of knowledge should be augmented with behavioural interventions to achieve longer-term change in self-care behaviours (3,23,25,46). Behavioural interventions had a larger effect size (ES) on self-management behaviours (ES −0.92) and on metabolic outcomes (ES 0.63) than knowledge-based or other psychological interventions (9). The more appropriate term may be "cognitive behavioural" interventions, which include cognitive restructuring, problem solving, cognitive-behavioural therapy (CBT), stress management, goal setting and relaxation. All

of these recognize that personal awareness and alteration of causative (possibly unconscious) thoughts and emotions are essential for effective behaviour change (47).

Several trials have found various cognitive-behavioural interventions to be effective in lowering A1C (4,15,48), improving QOL (49,50) and increasing self-care behaviours (15,23), whereas others have shown mixed results (3,46). Interventions that combine strategies for knowledge acquisition and self-care management (25,46) have been proven to be more effective in increasing knowledge, self-efficacy and self-care behaviours and in achieving metabolic control than programs that are didactic and knowledge oriented alone (4,9,15,51). Cognitive-behavioural interventions share common elements, including a patient-centred approach, shared decision making, the development of problem-solving skills, and the use of action plans directed toward patient-chosen goals (23,25,52).

A trusting, collaborative patient-healthcare professional relationship is also important for improving self-care behaviours (4). Frequent communication is a key indicator for successful interventions, whether done by a multidisciplinary team in a hospital or a community setting (33,53). Effective patient-clinician communication may improve adherence to recommendations (54). Communication technologies, such as e-Health and telemedicine with videoconferencing and teletransmission of home glucose monitoring, show promise for delivering individualized messages over an extended time period (52). Using a combination of different instructional methods that consistently incorporate an interactive component has been found to have somewhat more favourable effects than didactic programs (9,53).

Family and social support has positively impacted metabolic control and self-care behaviours (32,33,55). In both type 1 and type 2 diabetes, interventions that have targeted the family's ability to cope with stress have resulted in fewer conflicts, and having partners involved in care has been found to impact glycemic control (55).

Family and culturally tailored interventions are particularly relevant in minority communities. Several RCTs and systematic reviews have demonstrated that culturally competent healthcare interventions have resulted in lower A1C levels and improvements in diabetes-related knowledge and QOL (32,33,49).

Both individual and group settings have been used for cognitive-behavioural interventions, but there is no definitive conclusion as to which setting is superior (9,23). In general, group settings have been found to be more effective for weight loss and short-term glycemic control, whereas group interventions combined with individual follow-up sessions have resulted in lower A1C levels than either setting alone (10). Connecting with community partners and other chronic care model programs has proven to be a successful adjunct to cognitive-behavioural interventions (49,52,56). RCTs have concluded that different behavioural strategies are needed at different times to sustain behaviour change in the long term (56,57).

SME reinforcers and technological innovation

Incorporating booster sessions enhances the effectiveness of SME interventions (9). While healthcare providers play an essential role in SME delivery, patients are largely responsible for the majority of their own diabetes management. Historically, healthcare providers have been challenged with providing continued self-management support between visits. More recently, however, the availability of several different technologies (e.g. the internet, web-based education, text messaging [58–62], email, automatic telephone reminders [63], telehealth/telephone education [64–67] and reinforcement [68–72]) has provided an effective and time-efficient means of providing this ongoing support.

Several small trials have demonstrated improved outcomes when utilizing these technologies, reminder systems and

Healthcare provider tools/interventions	Patient roles
Booster sessions with varying behavioural strategies & ongoing support with: • Scheduled follow-up • Technology-enabled strategies • Reminder systems	Participate in monitoring health parameters Actively participate in technology-enabled and/or scheduled follow-up.
A **realistic** action plan for 1 or more self-care changes at a time. Include strategies to address barriers. Problem–solving exercises or applications for daily self-care decisions about monitoring, healthy food choices, medication, and exercise appropriate to treatment. Low literacy & numeracy materials & content. Personalized in-person contact may be more successful. Culturally appropriate materials. Peer or CHW may contribute to success for ethnic populations. Group and/or individual sessions are both appropriate for type 2 diabetes. Individual sessions may be superior for insulin education.	Collaborate on goals and decisions for a **realistic** action plan. Prioritize goals. Clarify barriers with providers; consider options to resolve. Inform provider of learning needs and preferences.
A collaborative trusting relationship. Effective communication skills, including motivational interviewing, to inform of risks, options, and to identify issues and/or barriers. Cognitive behavioural interventions which explore thoughts and feelings contributing to self-care behaviours. Assessment tools (e.g. PAID, self-care inventory) may be used. Low literacy/numeracy and culturally appropriate materials and communications. Personal connection with provider.	Identify and articulate the importance of own personal self-management needs/issues. Be open to exploration of thoughts and feelings underlying self-care decisions. Consider all options for action in context of individual pros and cons.
PATIENT–CENTERED CARE	

Steps (bottom to top):
- Evaluate and support long-term self-management
- Implement a realistic plan for skills training
- Collaborate on decisions and goals for action
- Make informed consideration of self-care options
- Assess and identify personal self-management needs

Figure 1. Steps to success in SME.
CHW, community health worker. *PAID*, Problem Areas In Diabetes scale.

scheduled follow-ups compared to controls. Outcomes include increased frequency of SMBG (58,63,71), improved adherence to treatment algorithms (31), improved self-efficacy (64–66) and QOL (70), as well as improved clinical outcomes, including reductions in A1C (59–62,65,69,73) and weight (67,68). However, 1 study of online diabetes education found no improvement in outcomes with the use of reinforcement methods (74).

A meta-analysis of studies examining the use of telemonitoring, home monitoring, telecare and telemedicine demonstrated a significant impact at the behavioural, clinical and structural levels (75). These strategies also resulted in significant reductions in A1C and diabetes-related complications, patient empowerment and improved patient understanding. However, the magnitude of the effect varied across studies and appeared to be dependent on the background characteristics of the patient population (e.g. ability for self-management, medical condition), sample selection and the approach to the treatment of control subjects.

Professional and peer delivery

Peer facilitators may augment multidisciplinary team practices in providing SME and/or social support, especially when developed as culturally relevant behavioural interventions for underserved populations (35). Two studies of the 6-week Diabetes Self-Management Program (DSMP) demonstrated the feasibility, but mixed effectiveness, of peer delivery of this standardized diabetes education program in Hispanic (71) and non-Hispanic populations (76). The DSMP was associated with significant A1C reductions in the Hispanic group (−0.4%) but not in the non-Hispanic group. Significant improvements in other outcomes, including decreased health distress, improved global health, decreased depressive

symptoms, improved self-efficacy and improved communication with physicians, were noted in both groups (71,76). In another study, a culturally tailored outreach and education program delivered by trained community health workers (CHW) was associated with significant improvements in self-care behaviours and similar A1C reductions compared to nurse-led case management and standard clinic care (77). Of note, the dropout rate was significantly lower in the CHW group (28% vs. 50% in the standard group), suggesting that the CHW may provide a trusted, culturally relevant and sustainable component to standard diabetes care (77).

The superiority of peer-delivered programs over similar programs delivered by health professionals has not been demonstrated in general populations with type 2 diabetes. A large study found that a peer-support intervention (i.e. 9 group sessions over 2 years) was not effective when targeted at all patients with type 2 diabetes (78). Another large study comparing specialist (nurse and physician) delivery to peer delivery of a 6-week, structured, interactive diabetes education program found no significant differences in either knowledge or A1C outcomes between the groups. However, the specialist group scored significantly higher in process and participant evaluations (79). Studies of the incremental effect of peer educators show much variability in terms of behaviour change and clinical outcomes (80,81). The specifics of training requirements for peer educators have not been clarified, and significant variations in training, scope of practice and issues of governance remain.

Delivery

No particular delivery strategy (e.g. video, web-based/online, phone, face-to-face, mixed) appears to result in consistently superior outcomes in persons with type 2 diabetes; however, larger effect sizes have been noted with strategies that involve personal contact with healthcare providers, either via face-to-face interactions or by telephone (9). A combination of didactic and interactive teaching methods, as well as group and individual sessions, appears to be most effective for persons with type 2 diabetes (9).

Conclusions

Since 2004, there has been a clear increase in the use of multifaceted programs that incorporate behavioural/psychosocial interventions, as well as knowledge and skills training, with a marked reduction in didactic educational programs that focus on knowledge or skill acquisition only (3). Interventions that include face-to-face delivery, a cognitive-behavioural method and the practical application of content are more likely to improve glycemic control (11,48). The most effective behavioural interventions involve a patient-centred approach, shared decision making, the enablement of problem-solving skills and the use of action plans directed toward patient-chosen goals. Steps to success in SME are summarized in Figure 1.

RECOMMENDATIONS

1. People with diabetes should be offered timely diabetes education that is tailored to enhance self-care practices and behaviours [Grade A, Level 1A (3,11,53)].

2. All people with diabetes who are able should be taught how to self-manage their diabetes [Grade A, Level 1A (53)].

3. SME that incorporates cognitive-behavioural educational interventions, such as problem solving, goal setting, and self-monitoring of health parameters, should be implemented for all individuals with diabetes [Grade B, Level 2 (11,23,48,82)].

4. Interventions that increase patient participation and collaboration in healthcare decision making should be used by providers [Grade B, Level 2 (53)].

5. For people with type 2 diabetes, SME interventions should be offered in small group and/or one-on-one settings, since both may be effective [Grade A, Level 1A (83,84)].

6. In both type 1 and 2 diabetes, interventions that target families' ability to cope with stress or diabetes-related conflict should be included in educational interventions when indicated [Grade B, Level 2 (55)].

7. Technologically based home blood glucose monitoring systems may be integrated into SME interventions in order to improve glycemic control [Grade C, Level 3 (75,85)].

8. Culturally appropriate SME, which may include peer or lay educators, may be used to increase diabetes-related knowledge and self-care behaviours and to decrease A1C [Grade B, Level 2 (32,34,77)].

9. Adding literacy- and numeracy-sensitive materials to a comprehensive diabetes management and education program may be used to improve knowledge, self-efficacy and A1C outcomes for patients with low literacy [Grade C, Level 3 (36)].

Abbreviations:
A1C, glycated hemoglobin; *SME,* self-management education.

Other Relevant Guidelines

References

1. Chodosh J, Morton SC, Mojica W, et al. Meta-analysis: chronic diseases self-management programs for older adults. Ann Intern Med 2005;143:427–58.
2. Bodenheimer T, Lorig K, Holman H, et al. Patient self-management of chronic disease in primary care. JAMA 2001;288:3470–5.
3. Minet L, Moller S, Lach V, et al. Mediating the effect of self-care management intervention in type 2 diabetes: a meta-analysis of 47 randomised controlled trials. Patient Educ Couns 2010;80:29–41.
4. Gary T, Genkinger J, Guallar E, et al. Meta-analysis of randomized educational and behavioral interventions in type 2 diabetes. Diabetes Educ 2003;29:488–501.
5. Cochrane J, Conn VS. Meta-analysis of quality of life outcomes following self-management training. Diabetes Educ 2008;34:815–23.
6. Look AHEAD Research group. Long-term effects of a lifestyle intervention on weight and cardiovascular risk factors in individuals with type 2 diabetes mellitus: four-year results of the Look AHEAD trial. Arch Intern Med 2010;170:1566–74.
7. Boren SA, Gunlock TL, Schaefer J, et al. Reducing risks in diabetes self-management: a systematic review of the literature. Diabetes Educ 2007;33:1053–77.
8. Hornsten A, Stenlund H, Lundman B, Sandstrom H. Improvements in HbA1c remain after 5 years: a follow up of an educational intervention focusing on patients' personal understandings of type 2 diabetes. Diabetes Res Clin Pract 2008;81:50–5.
9. Fan L, Sidani S. Effectiveness of diabetes self-management education intervention elements: a meta-analysis. Can J Diabetes 2009;33:18–26.
10. Norris SL, Lau J, Smith CH, et al. Self-management education for adults with type 2 diabetes: a meta-analysis of the effect on glycemic control. Diabetes Care 2002;25:1159–71.
11. Ellis S, Speroff T, Dittus R, et al. Diabetes patient education: a meta analysis and meta-regression. Patient Educ Couns 2004;52:97–105.
12. Wolfe S, Glasgow RE, Krist A, et al. Putting it together: finding success in behavior change through integration of services. Ann Fam Med 2005;3(suppl 2):s20–7.
13. Hill-Briggs F, Gemmell L. Problem solving in diabetes self-management and control: a systematic review of the literature. Diabetes Educ 2007;33:1032–50.
14. Funnell M, Nwankwo R, Gillard ML, et al. Implementing an empowerment-based diabetes self-management education program. Diabetes Educ 2005;31:53–6.
15. Ismail K, Maissi E, Thomas S, et al. A randomised controlled trial of cognitive behaviour therapy and motivational interviewing for people with type 1 diabetes mellitus with persistent sub-optimal glycemic control: a diabetes and psychological therapies study. Health Technol Assess 2010;14:1–101.
16. Polonsky W, Fisher L, Earles J, et al. Assessing psychosocial distress in diabetes: development of the diabetes distress scale. Diabetes Care 2005;28:626–31.
17. Weinger K, Butler H, Welch G, LaGreca A. measuring diabetes self-care: a psychometric analysis of the Self-Care Inventory-revised with adults. Diabetes Care 2005;28:1346–52.
18. Toobert D, Hampson S, Glasgow R. The Summary of Diabetes Self-Care Activities measure: results from 7 studies and a revised scale. Diabetes Care 2000;23:943–55.
19. Sigurdardottir A, Benediktsson R, Jonsdottir H. Instruments to tailor care of people with diabetes. J Adv Nurs 2009;65:2118–30.
20. Canadian Diabetes Association. In: Jones H, editor. Building Competency in Diabetes Education: The Essentials. Toronto, ON: Canadian Diabetes Association; 2008.
21. American Association of Diabetes Educators. Standards for outcome measures of diabetes self-management. Diabetes Educ 2003;29:804–16.
22. Scain SF, Friedman R, Gross JL. A structured educational program improves metabolic control in patients with type 2 diabetes: a randomized controlled trial. Diabetes Educ 2009;35:603–11.
23. Kulzer B, Hermanns N, Reinhecker H, et al. Effects of self-management training in type 2 diabetes: a randomized prospective trial. Diabetic Med 2007;24:415–23.
24. Sturt JA, Whitlock S, Fox C, et al. Effects of the Diabetes Manual 1:1 structured education in primary care. Diabet Med 2008;25:722–31.
25. Davies MJ, Heller S, Skinner TC, et al. Effectiveness of the diabetes education and self-management for ongoing and newly diagnosed (DESMOND) programme for people with newly diagnosed type 2 diabetes: cluster randomised controlled trial. BMJ 2008;336:491–5.
26. Wattana C, Srisuphan W, Pothiban L, et al. Effects of a diabetes self-management program on glycemic control, coronary heart disease risk, and quality of life among Thai patients with type 2 diabetes. Nurs Health Sci 2007;9:135–41.
27. Christian J, Bessesen D, Byers T, et al. Clinic based support to help overweight patients with type 2 diabetes increase physical activity and lose weight. Arch Intern Med 2008;168:141–6.
28. Wens J, Vermeire E, Hearnshaw H, et al. Educational interventions aiming at improving adherence to treatment recommendations in type 2 diabetes: a sub-analysis of a systematic review of randomised controlled trials. Diabetes Res Clin Pract 2008;79:377–88.
29. Dutton G, Provost B, Tan F, et al. A tailored print-based physical activity intervention for patients with type 2 diabetes. Prev Med 2008;47:409–11.
30. Chen HS, Wu TE, Jap TS, et al. Improvement of glycaemia control in subjects with type 2 diabetes by self-monitoring of blood glucose: comparison of two

management programs adjusting bedtime insulin dosage. Diabetes Obes Metab 2008;10:34–40.

31. Dyson PA, Beatty S, Matthews DR. An assessment of lifestyle video education for people newly diagnosed with type 2 diabetes. J Hum Nutr Diet 2008;23: 353–9.

32. Whittemore R. Culturally competent interventions for Hispanic adults with type 2 diabetes: a systematic review. J Transcult Nurs 2007;18:157–66.

33. Samuel-Hodge C, Keyserling T, Park S, et al. A randomized trial of a church-based diabetes self-management program for African Americans with type 2 diabetes. Diabetes Educ 2009;35:439–54.

34. Hawthorne K, Robles Y, Cannings-John R, et al. Culturally appropriate health education for type 2 diabetes in ethnic minority groups: a systematic and narrative review of randomized control trials. Diabet Med 2010;27:613–23.

35. Lujan J, Ostwald S, Ortiz M. Promotora diabetes intervention for Mexican Americans. Diabetes Educ 2007;33:660–70.

36. Van Scoyoc EF, deWalt DA. Interventions to Improve diabetes outcomes for people with low literacy and numeracy: a systematic literature review. Diabetes Spectrum 2010;23:228–37.

37. Cavenaugh K, Wallston KA, Gerretsadik T, et al. Addressing literacy and numeracy to improve diabetes care. Diabetes Care 2009;32:2149–55.

38. Osborn C, Cavenaugh K, Wallston KA, et al. Diabetes Numeracy: an overlooked factor in understanding racial disparities in glycemic control. Diabetes Care 2009;32:1614–9.

39. Borges WJ, Ostwald SK. Improving foot self-care behaviors with Pies Sanos. West J Nurs Res 2008;30:325–41.

40. Duran A, Martin P, Runkle I, et al. Benefits of self-monitoring blood glucose in the management of new-onset type 2 diabetes mellitus: the St. Carlos Study, a prospective randomized clinic-based interventional study with parallel groups. J Diabetes 2010;2:203–11.

41. Farmer AJ, Wade AN, French DP, et al. Blood glucose self-monitoring in type 2 diabetes: a randomised controlled trial. Health Technol Assess 2009;13: iii-iv, ix-xi,1–50.

42. Moriyama M, Nakano M, Kuroe Y, et al. Efficacy of a self-management education program for people with type 2 diabetes: results of a 12 month trial. Jpn J Nurs Sci 2009;6:51–63.

43. Skelly AH, Carlson J, Leeman J, et al. Controlled trial of nursing interventions to improve health outcomes of older African American women with type 2 diabetes. Nurs Res 2009;58:410–8.

44. Yki-Jarvinen H, Juurinen L, Alvarsson M, et al. Initiate insulin by aggressive titration and education (INITIATE): a randomized study to compare initiation of insulin combination therapy in type 2 diabetic patients individually and in groups. Diabetes Care 2007;30:1364–9.

45. Krousel-Wood MA, Berger L, Jiang X, et al. Does home-based exercise improve body mass index in patients with type 2 diabetes? Results of a feasibility trial. Diabetes Res Clin Pract 2008;79:230–6.

46. Magwood G, Zapka J, Jenkins C. A review of systematic reviews evaluating diabetes interventions. Focus on quality of life and disparities. Diabetes Educ 2008;34:242–65.

47. Ismail K, Winkley K, Rae-Hesketh S. Systematic review and meta-analysis of randomized controlled trials of psychological interventions to improve glycaemic control in patients with type 2 diabetes. Lancet 2004;363:1589–97.

48. Weinger K, Beverly E, Lee Y, et al. The effect of a structured behavioral intervention in poorly controlled diabetes. Arch Intern Med 2011;171:1990–8.

49. Kim M, Han H, Song H, et al. A community-based, culturally tailored behavioral intervention for Korean Americans with type 2 diabetes. Diabetes Educ 2009; 35:986–94.

50. Toobert D, Glasgow R, Strycker L, et al. Long-term effects of the Mediterranean lifestyle program: a randomized clinical trial for postmenopausal women with type 2 diabetes. Int J Behav Nutr Phys Act 2007;4:1479–81.

51. Mulcahy K, Maryniuk M, Peeples M, et al. Diabetes self-management education core outcomes measures. Diabetes Educ 2003;29:768–803.

52. Gambling T, Long A. The realisation of patient-centered care during a 3 year proactive telephone counselling self-care intervention for diabetes. Patient Educ Couns 2010;80:219–26.

53. Norris SL, Engelgau MM, Narayan KMV. Effectiveness of self-management training in type 2 diabetes: a systematic review of randomized controlled trials. Diabetes Care 2001;24:561–87.

54. Nam S, Chesla C, Stotts NA, et al. Barriers to diabetes management: patient and provider factors. Diabetes Res Clin Pract 2011;923:1–9.

55. Armour TA, Norris SL, Jack Jr L, et al. The effectiveness of family interventions in people with diabetes mellitus: a systematic review. Diabet Med 2005;22: 1295–305.

56. Piatt G, Anderson R, Brooks M, et al. 3-Year follow-up of clinical and behavioural improvements following a multifaceted diabetes care intervention: results of a randomized controlled trial. Diabetes Educ 2010;36:301–9.

57. Thoolen B, Ridder D, Bensing J, et al. Beyond good intentions: the role of proactive coping in achieving sustained behavioural change in the context of diabetes management. Psychol Health 2009;24:237–54.

58. Hanauer DA, Wentzell K, Laffel N, et al. Computerized automated reminder diabetes system (CARDS): e-mail and SMS cell phone text messaging reminders to support diabetes management. Diabetes Technol Ther 2009;11: 99–106.

59. Yoon KH, Kim HS. A short message service by cellular phone in type 2 diabetic patients for 12 months. Diabetes Res Clin Pract 2008;79:256–61.

60. Kim HS. A randomized controlled trial of a nurse short-message service by cellular phone for people with diabetes. Int J Nurs Stud 2007;44:687–92.

61. Kim HS, Jeong HS. A nurse short message service by cellular phone in type-2 diabetic patients for six months. J Clin Nurs 2007;16:1082–7.

62. Kim HS, Song MS. Technological intervention for obese patients with type 2 diabetes. Appl Nurs Res 2008;21:84–9.

63. Graziano JA, Gross CR. A randomized controlled trial of an automated telephone intervention to improve glycemic control in type 2 diabetes. Adv Nurs Sci 2009;32:E42–57.

64. Weinstock RS, Brooks G, Palmas W, et al. Lessened decline in physical activity and impairment of older adults with diabetes with telemedicine and pedometer use: results from the IDEATel study. Age Ageing 2008;40:98–105.

65. Trief PM, Teresi JA, Eimicke JP, et al. Improvement in diabetes self-efficacy and glycaemic control using telemedicine in a sample of older, ethnically diverse individuals who have diabetes: the IDEATel project. Age Ageing 2009;38: 219–25.

66. Trief PM, Teresi JA, Izquierdo R, et al. Psychosocial outcomes of telemedicine case management for elderly patients with diabetes: the randomized IDEATel trial. Diabetes Care 2007;30:1266–8.

67. Franciosi M, Lucisano G, Pellegrini F. ROSES: role of self-monitoring of blood glucose and Intensive education in patients with type 2 diabetes not receiving insulin. A pilot randomized clinical trial. Diabet Med 2011;28:789–96.

68. Wu L, Forbes A, White A. Patients' experience of a telephone booster intervention to support weight management in type 2 diabetes and its acceptability. J Telemed Telecare 2010;16:221–3.

69. Stone RA, Rao RH, Sevick MA, et al. Active care management supported by home telemonitoring in veterans with type 2 diabetes: the DiaTel randomized controlled trial. Diabetes Care 2010;33:478–84.

70. Jansa M, Vidal M, Viaplana J, et al. Telecare in a structured therapeutic education programme addressed to patients with type 1 diabetes and poor metabolic control. Diabetes Res Clin Pract 2006;74:26–32.

71. Lorig K, Ritter PL, Villa F, et al. Spanish diabetes self-management with and without automated telephone reinforcement. Diabetes Care 2008;31: 408–13.

72. Walker E, Shmukler C, Ullman R. Results of a successful telephonic intervention to improve diabetes control in urban adults: a randomized trial. Diabetes Care 2011;34:2–7.

73. Pare G, Moqadem K, Pineau G, et al. Clinical effects of home telemonitoring in the context of diabetes, asthma, heart failure and hypertension: a systematic review. J Med Internet Res 2010;12:e21.

74. Lorig K, Ritter PL, Laurent DD, et al. Online diabetes self-management program: a randomized study. Diabetes Care 2010;33:1275–81.

75. Jaana M, Pare G. Home telemonitoring of patients with diabetes: a systematic assessment of observed effects. J Eval Clin Pract 2007;13:242–53.

76. Lorig K, Ritter PL, Villa FJ, et al. Community-based peer-led diabetes self-management: a randomized trial. Diabetes Educ 2009;35:641–51.

77. Babamato K, Sey KA, Karlan V, et al. Improving diabetes care and health measures among Hispanics using community health workers: results from a randomized controlled trial. Health Educ Behav 2009;36:113–26.

78. Smith SM, Paul G, Kelly A, et al. Peer support for patients with type 2 diabetes: cluster randomised controlled trial. BMJ 2011;342:d715.

79. Baksi AK, Al-Mrayat M, Hogan D, et al. Peer advisers compared with specialist health professionals in delivering a training programme on self-management to people with diabetes: a randomised controlled trial. Diabet Med 2008;25: 1076–82.

80. Norris SL, Chowdhury FM, Van Le K, et al. Effectiveness of community health workers in the care of persons with diabetes. Diabetic Med 2006;23: 544–56.

81. Perez-Escamilla R, Hromi-Fiedler A, Vega-Lopez S, et al. Impact of peer nutrition education on dietary behaviors and health outcomes among Latinos: a systematic literature review. J Nutr Educ Behav 2008;40:208–25.

82. Steed L, Cooke D, Newman S. A systematic review of psychosocial outcomes following education, self-management and psychological interventions in diabetes mellitus. Patient Educ Couns 2003;51:5–15.

83. Rickheim PL, Weaver TW, Flader JL, et al. Assessment of group versus individual diabetes education: a randomized study. Diabetes Care 2002;25:269–74.

84. Deakin T, McShane CE, Cade JE, et al. Group based training for self-management strategies in people with type 2 diabetes mellitus. Cochrane Database System Rev 2005;2:CD003417.

85. Tildesley HD, Mazanderani AB, Ross SA. Effect of internet therapeutic intervention on A1C levels in patients with type 2 diabetes treated with insulin. Diabetes Care 2010;33:1738–40.

61

Table 1. Types of Insulin

INSULIN TYPE (TRADE NAME)	ONSET	PEAK	DURATION
Bolus (prandial) insulins			
Rapid-acting insulin analogues (clear) • Insulin aspart (NovoRapid®) • Insulin glulisine (Apidra®) • Insulin lispro (Humalog®)	10 – 15 min 10 – 15 min 10 – 15 min	1 – 1.5 h 1 – 1.5 h 1 – 2 h	3 – 5 h 3 – 5 h 3.5 – 4.75 h
Short-acting insulins (clear) • Humulin®-R • Novolin® ge Toronto	30 min	2 – 3 h	6.5 h
Basal insulins			
Intermediate-acting (cloudy) • Humulin® -N • Novolin® ge NPH	1 – 3 h	5 – 8 h	Up to 18 h
Long-acting insulin (clear) • Insulin detemir (Levemir®) • Insulin glargine (Lantus®) • Insulin glargine U300 (Toujeo®)	90 min 90 min Up to 6 h	Not applicable	Up to 24h (detemir 16-24 h) Up to 24h (glargine 24 h) Up to 30 h
Premixed insulins			
Premixed regular insulin –NPH (cloudy) • Humulin® 30/70 • Novolin® ge 30/70, 40/60, 50/50	A single vial or cartridge contains a fixed ratio of insulin (% of rapid-acting or short-acting insulin to % of intermediate-acting insulin)		
Premixed insulin analogues (cloudy) • Biphasic insulin aspart (NovoMix® 30) • Insulin lispro/lispro protamine (Humalog®Mix25 and Mix50)			

Note: Pork regular insulin (Hypurin Regular Insulin Pork) and pork isophane insulin (Hypurin NPH Insulin Isophane) are available but rarely used.

Physicians should refer to the most current edition of *Compendium of Pharmaceuticals and Specialties* (Canadian Pharmacists Association; Ottawa, Ontario, Canada) and product monographs for detailed information.

Can J Diabetes 37 (2013) S153–S162

Contents lists available at SciVerse ScienceDirect

Canadian Journal of Diabetes

journal homepage:
www.canadianjournalofdiabetes.com

Clinical Practice Guidelines

Type 1 Diabetes in Children and Adolescents

Canadian Diabetes Association Clinical Practice Guidelines Expert Committee

The initial draft of this chapter was prepared by Diane Wherrett MD, FRCPC, Céline Huot MD, MSc, FRCPC, Beth Mitchell PhD, Cpsych, Danièle Pacaud MD, FRCPC

KEY MESSAGES

- Suspicion of diabetes in a child should lead to immediate confirmation of the diagnosis and initiation of treatment to reduce the likelihood of diabetic ketoacidosis (DKA).
- Management of pediatric DKA differs from DKA in adults because of the increased risk for cerebral edema. Pediatric protocols should be used.
- Children should be referred for diabetes education, ongoing care and psychosocial support to a diabetes team with pediatric expertise.

Note: Unless otherwise specified, the term "child" or "children" is used for individuals 0 to 18 years of age, and the term "adolescent" for those 13 to 18 years of age.

Introduction

Diabetes mellitus is the most common endocrine disease and one of the most common chronic conditions in children. Type 2 diabetes and other types of diabetes, including genetic defects of beta cell function, such as maturity-onset diabetes of the young, are being increasingly recognized in children and should be considered when clinical presentation is atypical for type 1 diabetes. This section addresses those areas of type 1 diabetes management that are specific to children.

Education

Children with new-onset type 1 diabetes and their families require intensive diabetes education by an interdisciplinary pediatric diabetes healthcare (DHC) team to provide them with the necessary skills and knowledge to manage this disease. The complex physical, developmental and emotional needs of children and their families necessitate specialized care to ensure the best long-term outcomes (1,2). Education topics must include insulin action and administration, dosage adjustment, blood glucose (BG) and ketone testing, sick-day management and prevention of diabetic ketoacidosis (DKA), nutrition therapy, exercise, and prevention, detection, and treatment of hypoglycemia. Anticipatory guidance and lifestyle counselling should be part of routine care, especially during critical developmental transitions (e.g. upon school entry, beginning high school). Healthcare providers should regularly initiate discussions with children and their families about

school, diabetes camp, psychological issues, substance use, obtaining a driver's license and career choices.

Children with new-onset diabetes who present with DKA require a short period of hospitalization to stabilize the associated metabolic derangements and to initiate insulin therapy. Outpatient education for children with new-onset diabetes has been shown to be less expensive than inpatient education and associated with similar or slightly better outcomes when appropriate resources are available (3).

Glycemic Targets

As improved metabolic control reduces both the onset and progression of diabetes-related complications in adults and adolescents with type 1 diabetes (4,5), aggressive attempts should be made to reach the recommended glycemic targets outlined in Table 1. However, clinical judgement is required to determine which children can reasonably and safely achieve these targets. Treatment goals and strategies must be tailored to each child, with consideration given to individual risk factors. Young age at diabetes onset ($<$7 years of age) has been associated with poorer cognitive function in many studies (6). Episodes of severe hypoglycemia have been associated with poorer cognitive function in some follow-up studies, while other studies have found chronic hyperglycemia in young children to be associated with poorer cognitive performance (7–10). Analysis from a large multicentre observational study found that knowledge of glycemic targets by patients and parents, and consistent target setting by the diabetes team, was associated with improved metabolic control (11).

Insulin Therapy

Insulin therapy is the mainstay of medical management of type 1 diabetes. A variety of insulin regimens can be used, but few have been studied specifically in children with new-onset diabetes. The choice of insulin regimen depends on many factors, including the child's age, duration of diabetes, family lifestyle, socioeconomic factors, and family, patient, and physician preferences. Regardless of the insulin regimen used, all children should be treated to meet glycemic targets.

The honeymoon period, which can last up to 2 years after diagnosis, is characterized by good glycemic control and low insulin requirements ($<$0.5 units/kg/day). At the end of this period, more

1499-2671/$ – see front matter © 2013 Canadian Diabetes Association
http://dx.doi.org/10.1016/j.jcjd.2013.01.042

65

Table 1
Recommended glycemic targets for children and adolescents with type 1 diabetes

Age (years)	A1C (%)	Fasting/preprandial PG (mmol/L)	Two-hour postprandial PG* (mmol/L)	Considerations
<6	<8.0	6.0–10.0	—	Caution is required to minimize hypoglycemia because of the potential association between severe hypoglycemia and later cognitive impairment. Consider target of <8.5% if excessive hypoglycemia occurs
6–12	≤7.5	4.0–10.0	—	Targets should be graduated to the child's age. Consider target of <8.0% if excessive hypoglycemia occurs.
13–18	≤7.0	4.0–7.0	5.0–10.0	Appropriate for most adolescents.[†]

A1C, glycated hemoglobin; *PG*, plasma glucose.
  * Postprandial monitoring is rarely done in young children except for those on pump therapy for whom targets are not available.
  [†] In adolescents in whom it can be safely achieved, consider aiming toward normal PG range (i.e. A1C ≤6.0%, fasting/preprandial PG 4.0–6.0 mmol/L and 2-hour postprandial PG 5.0–8.0 mmol/L).

intensive management may be required to continue meeting glycemic targets. Two methods of intensive diabetes management have been used: basal-bolus regimens (long-acting basal insulin analogues and rapid-acting bolus insulin analogues) and continuous subcutaneous insulin infusion (CSII; insulin pump therapy). Basal-bolus therapy has resulted in improved control over traditional twice daily NPH and rapid-acting bolus analogue therapy in some but not all studies (12,13). CSII is safe and effective and can be initiated at any age (14). A Cochrane review found that CSII gave slightly improved metabolic control over basal-bolus therapy (15). Some clinic-based studies of CSII in school-aged children and adolescents have shown a significant reduction in glycated hemoglobin (A1C) with reduced hypoglycemia 12 to 24 months after initiation of CSII when compared to pre-CSII levels (16). CSII, with use of a continuous glucose sensor, resulted in improved control over basal-bolus therapy alone (17). Most, but not all, pediatric studies of the long-acting basal insulin analogues, detemir and glargine, have demonstrated improved fasting BG levels and fewer episodes of nocturnal hypoglycemia with a reduction in A1C (12,18–20). Two large population-based observational studies have not found improved A1C in patients using basal-bolus therapy or CSII when compared to those using NPH and rapid-acting bolus analogues (21,22). Individualization of insulin therapy to reach A1C targets, minimize hypoglycemia and optimize quality of life is indicated.

Glucose Monitoring

Self-monitoring of BG is an essential part of management of type 1 diabetes (23). Subcutaneous continuous glucose sensors allow detection of asymptomatic hypoglycemia and hyperglycemia. Use has resulted in improved diabetes control with less hypoglycemia in some studies. A randomized controlled trial did not show improved control in children and adolescents but did in adults (24). Benefit correlated with duration of sensor use, which was much lower in children and adolescents.

Nutrition

All children with type 1 diabetes should receive counselling from a registered dietitian experienced in pediatric diabetes. Children with diabetes should follow a healthy diet as recommended for children without diabetes in *Eating Well with Canada's Food Guide* (25). This involves consuming a variety of foods from the 4 food groups (grain products, vegetables and fruits, milk and alternatives, and meat and alternatives). There is no evidence that 1 form of nutrition therapy is superior to another in attaining age-appropriate glycemic targets. Appropriate matching of insulin to carbohydrate content may allow increased flexibility and improved glycemic control (26,27), but the use of insulin to carbohydrate ratios is not required. The effect of protein and fat on glucose

absorption must also be considered. Nutrition therapy should be individualized (based on the child's nutritional needs, eating habits, lifestyle, ability and interest) and must ensure normal growth and development without compromising glycemic control. This plan should be evaluated regularly and at least annually. Features suggestive of eating disorders and of celiac disease should be systematically sought out (28).

Hypoglycemia

Hypoglycemia is a major obstacle for children with type 1 diabetes and can affect their ability to achieve glycemic targets. Children with early-onset diabetes are at greatest risk for disruption of cognitive function and neuropsychological skills, but the respective roles of hypoglycemia and hyperglycemia in their development are still questioned (6,29). Significant risk of hypoglycemia often necessitates less stringent glycemic goals, particularly for younger children. There is no evidence in children that 1 insulin regimen or mode of administration is superior to another for resolving non-severe hypoglycemia. As such, treatment must be individualized (30). Frequent use of continuous glucose monitoring in a clinical care setting may reduce episodes of hypoglycemia (31). Severe hypoglycemia should be treated with pediatric doses of intravenous (IV) dextrose in the hospital setting or glucagon in the home setting. In children, the use of mini-doses of glucagon has been shown to be useful in the home management of mild or impending hypoglycemia associated with inability or refusal to take oral carbohydrate. A dose of 10 μg per year of age (minimum dose 20 μg, maximum dose 150 μg) is effective at treating and preventing hypoglycemia, with an additional doubled dose given if the BG has not increased in 20 minutes (32,33). See Table 2 for treatment of mild-to-moderate hypoglycemia.

Chronic Poor Metabolic Control

Diabetes control may worsen during adolescence. Factors responsible for this deterioration include adolescent adjustment issues, psychosocial distress, intentional insulin omission and physiological insulin resistance. A careful multidisciplinary assessment should be undertaken for every child with chronic poor metabolic control (e.g. A1C >10.0%) to identify potential causative

Table 2
Examples of carbohydrate for treatment of mild-to-moderate hypoglycemia

	<15 kg	15–30 kg	>30 kg
Patient weight			
Amount of carbohydrate	5 g	10 g	15 g
Carbohydrate source			
Glucose tablet (4 g)	1	2 or 3	4
Dextrose tablet (3 g)	2	3	5
Apple or orange juice, regular soft drink, sweet beverage (cocktails)	40 mL	85 mL	125 mL

factors, such as depression and eating disorders, and to identify and address barriers to improved control. Multipronged interventions that target emotional, family and coping issues show a modest reduction in A1C with reduced rates of hospital admission (34,35).

DKA

DKA occurs in 15% to 67% of children with new-onset diabetes and at a frequency of 1 to 10 episodes per 100 patient years in those with established diabetes (36). As DKA is the leading cause of morbidity and mortality in children with diabetes, strategies are required to prevent the development of DKA (37). In new-onset diabetes, DKA can be prevented through earlier recognition and initiation of insulin therapy. Public awareness campaigns about the early signs of diabetes have significantly reduced the frequency of DKA in new-onset diabetes (38). In children with established diabetes, DKA results from failing to take insulin or poor sick-day management. Risk is increased in children with poor metabolic control or previous episodes of DKA, peripubertal and adolescent girls, children on insulin pumps or long-acting basal insulin analogues, children with psychiatric disorders and those with difficult family circumstances (39–41). The frequency of DKA in established diabetes can be decreased with education, behavioural intervention and family support (42,43), as well as access to 24-hour telephone services for parents of children with diabetes (44,45).

Management of DKA

While most cases of DKA are corrected without event, 0.7% to 3.0% of pediatric cases are complicated by cerebral edema (CE) (46), which is associated with significant morbidity (21% to 35%) and mortality (21% to 24%) (47). In contrast, CE has rarely been reported in adults (39,47). Although the cause of CE is still unknown, several factors are associated with increased risk (Table 3) (48–52). A bolus of insulin prior to infusion is not recommended since it does not offer faster resolution of acidosis (53,54) and may contribute to CE (55). Recent evidence suggests early insulin administration (within the first hour of fluid replacement) may increase the risk for CE (52). Special caution should be exercised in young children with DKA and new-onset diabetes or a greater degree of acidosis and extracellular fluid volume depletion because of the increased risk of CE. Use of bedside criteria may allow earlier identification of patients who require treatment for CE (56). DKA should be managed according to published protocols for management of pediatric DKA (Figure 1) (57).

Immunization

Historically, national guidelines have recommended influenza and pneumococcal immunization for children with type 1 diabetes (58–60). Currently, there is no evidence supporting increased morbidity or mortality from influenza or pneumococcus in children with type 1 diabetes (61,62). However, the management of type 1 diabetes can be complicated by illness, requiring parental knowledge of sick-day management and increased attention during periods of illness. For this reason, parents may choose to immunize their children. Long-lasting immunogenicity to influenza vaccination has been shown to be adequate in these children (63).

Smoking Prevention and Cessation

Smoking is a significant risk factor for both macrovascular and microvascular complications of diabetes (64) and, in adolescents, is associated with worse metabolic control (65). Smoking prevention should be emphasized throughout childhood and adolescence.

Table 3
Risk factors for cerebral edema

- Younger age (<5 years)
- New-onset diabetes
- High initial serum urea
- Low initial partial pressure of arterial carbon dioxide (pCO_2)
- Rapid administration of hypotonic fluids
- IV bolus of insulin
- Early IV insulin infusion (within first hour of administration of fluids)
- Failure of serum sodium to rise during treatment
- Use of bicarbonate

IV, intravenous.

Contraception and Sexual Health Counselling

Adolescents with diabetes should receive regular counselling about sexual health and contraception. Unplanned pregnancies should be avoided, as pregnancy in adolescent females with type 1 diabetes with suboptimal metabolic control may result in higher risks of maternal and fetal complications than in older women with type 1 diabetes who are already at increased risk compared to the general population (66).

Psychological Issues

For children, and particularly adolescents, there is a need to identify psychological disorders associated with diabetes and to intervene early to minimize the impact over the course of development.

Psychological/psychiatric risks

Children and adolescents with diabetes have significant risks for psychological problems, including depression, anxiety, eating disorders and externalizing disorders (67–69). The risks increase exponentially during adolescence (70,71). Studies have shown that psychological disorders predict poor diabetes management and control (72–75) and, consequently, negative medical outcomes (76–79). Conversely, as glycemic control worsens, the probability of psychological problems increases (80).

The presence of psychological symptoms and diabetes problems in children and adolescents are often strongly affected by caregiver/family distress. Research has demonstrated that while parental psychological issues may distort perceptions of the child's diabetes control (81), often, they are related to poor psychological adjustment and diabetes control (82–85). Maternal anxiety and depression are associated with poor diabetes control in younger adolescents and with reduced positive effect and motivation in older teens (86).

Eating disorders

Ten percent of adolescent females with type 1 diabetes meet the *Diagnostic and Statistical Manual of Mental Disorders* (4th Edition) criteria for eating disorders compared to 4% of their age-matched peers without diabetes (87). Furthermore, eating disorders are associated with poor metabolic control and earlier onset and more rapid progression of microvascular complications (88). Eating disorders should be suspected in those adolescent and young adult females who are unable to achieve and maintain metabolic targets, especially when insulin omission is suspected. It is important to identify individuals with eating disorders because different management strategies are required to optimize metabolic control and prevent microvascular complications (87–89).

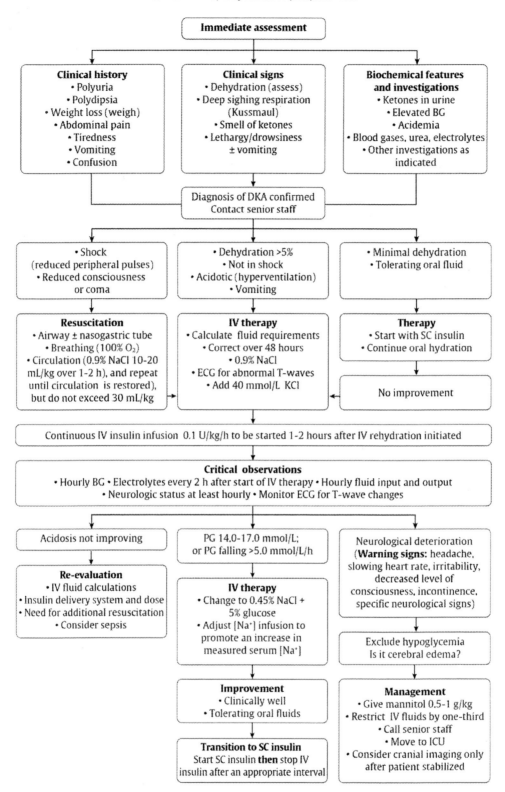

Figure 1. Immediate assessment and management of diabetic ketoacidosis (DKA) in children. *BG*, blood glucose; *ECG*, electrocardiogram; *ICU*, intensive care unit; *IV*, intravenous; *PG*, plasma glucose; *SC*, subcutaneous. Adapted with permission from 57. Wolfsdorf J, Craig ME, Daneman D, et al; for the International Society for Pediatric and Adolescent Diabetes. Diabetic ketoacidosis. Pediatr Diabetes. 2007;8:28-43.

Prevention and intervention

Children and adolescents with diabetes, along with their families, should be screened throughout their development for psychological disorders (90). Given the prevalence of psychological issues, screening in this area can be seen as equally important as screening for microvascular complications in children and adolescents with diabetes (91).

Psychological interventions with children and adolescents, as well as families, have been shown to improve mental health (67,92), including overall well-being and perceived quality of life (93), along with depressive symptoms (94,95). In addition, there is

Table 4
Recommendations for screening for comorbid conditions in children with type 1 diabetes

Condition	Indications for screening	Screening test	Frequency
Autoimmune thyroid disease	All children with type 1 diabetes	Serum TSH level + thyroperoxidase antibodies	At diagnosis and every 2 years thereafter
	Positive thyroid antibodies, thyroid symptoms or goiter	Serum TSH level + thyroperoxidase antibodies	Every 6–12 months
Addison's disease	Unexplained recurrent hypoglycemia and decreasing insulin requirements	8 AM serum cortisol + serum sodium and potassium	As clinically indicated
Celiac disease	Recurrent gastrointestinal symptoms, poor linear growth, poor weight gain, fatigue, anemia, unexplained frequent hypoglycemia or poor metabolic control	Tissue transglutaminase + immunoglobulin A levels	As clinically indicated

TSH, thyroid-stimulating hormone.

some evidence that psychosocial interventions can positively affect glycemic control (34,92,96). Most importantly, some studies have demonstrated that psychological interventions can increase both diabetes treatment adherence and glycemic control, as well as psychosocial functioning (97,98).

Comorbid Conditions

Autoimmune thyroid disease

Clinical autoimmune thyroid disease (AITD) occurs in 15% to 30% of individuals with type 1 diabetes (99). The risk for AITD during the first decade of diabetes is directly related to the presence or absence of thyroid antibodies at diabetes diagnosis (100). Hypothyroidism is most likely to develop in girls at puberty (101). Early detection and treatment of hypothyroidism will prevent growth failure and symptoms of hypothyroidism (Table 4). Hyperthyroidism also occurs more frequently in association with type 1 diabetes than in the general population.

Addison's disease

Addison's disease is rare, even in those with type 1 diabetes (102). Targeted screening is required in those with unexplained recurrent hypoglycemia and decreasing insulin requirements (Table 4).

Celiac disease

Celiac disease can be identified in 4% to 9% of children with type 1 diabetes (99), but in 60% to 70% of these children the disease is asymptomatic (silent celiac disease). Children with type 1 diabetes are at increased risk for classic or atypical celiac disease during the first 10 years of diabetes (103). There is good evidence that treatment of classic or atypical celiac disease with a gluten-free diet improves intestinal and extraintestinal symptoms (104) and prevents the long-term sequelae of untreated classic celiac disease (105). However, there is no evidence that untreated asymptomatic celiac disease is associated with short- or long-term health risks (106) or that a gluten-free diet improves health in these individuals (107). Thus, universal screening for and treatment of asymptomatic celiac disease remains controversial (Table 4).

Diabetes Complications

There are important age-related considerations regarding surveillance for diabetes complications and interpretation of investigations (Table 5).

Nephropathy

Prepubertal children and those in the first five years of diabetes should be considered at very low risk for microalbuminuria (108,109). A first morning urine albumin to creatinine ratio (ACR) has high sensitivity and specificity for the detection of microalbuminuria (110,111). Although screening with a random ACR is associated with greater compliance than with a first morning sample, its specificity may be compromised in adolescents due to their higher frequency of exercise-induced proteinuria and benign postural proteinuria. Abnormal random ACRs (>2.5 mg/mmol)

Table 5
Screening for diabetes complications, dyslipidemia and hypertension in children with type 1 diabetes

Complication	Indications and intervals for screening	Screening method
Nephropathy	• Yearly screening commencing at 12 years of age in those with duration of type 1 diabetes >5 years	• First morning (preferred) or random ACR • Abnormal ACR requires confirmation at least 1 month later with a first morning ACR and, if abnormal, followed by timed, overnight or 24-hour split urine collections for albumin excretion rate • Repeated sampling should be done every 3–4 months over a 12-month period to demonstrate persistence
Retinopathy	• Yearly screening commencing at 15 years of age with duration of type 1 diabetes >5 years • Screening interval can increase to 2 years if good glycemic control, duration of diabetes <10 years and no retinopathy at initial assessment	• Standard field, stereoscopic colour fundus photography with interpretation by a trained reader (gold standard), or • Direct ophthalmoscopy or indirect slit-lamp funduscopy through dilated pupil, or • Digital fundus photography
Neuropathy	• Postpubertal adolescents with poor metabolic control should be screened yearly after 5 years' duration of type 1 diabetes	• Question and examine for symptoms of numbness, pain, cramps and paraesthesia, as well as skin sensation, vibration sense, light touch and ankle reflexes
Dyslipidemia	• Delay screening after diabetes diagnosis until metabolic control has stabilized • Screen at 12 and 17 years of age • <12 years of age: screen only those with body mass index >95th percentile, family history of hyperlipidemia or premature cardiovascular disease	• Fasting total cholesterol, high-density lipoprotein cholesterol, triglycerides, calculated low-density lipoprotein cholesterol
Hypertension	• Screen all children with type 1 diabetes at least twice a year	• Use appropriate cuff size

ACR, albumin to creatinine ratio.

require confirmation with a first morning ACR or timed urine overnight collection (112).

Microalbuminuria is rare in prepubertal children, regardless of the duration of diabetes or metabolic control (108). Furthermore, the likelihood of transient or intermittent microalbuminuria is higher during the early peripubertal years (109). Individuals with transient or intermittent microalbuminuria may be at increased risk of progression to overt nephropathy (113). Abnormal screening results require confirmation and follow-up to demonstrate persistent abnormalities.

Treatment is indicated only for those adolescents with persistent microalbuminuria. One short-term randomized controlled trial in adolescents demonstrated that angiotensin-converting enzyme (ACE) inhibitors were effective in reducing microalbuminuria compared to placebo (114). However, there are no long-term intervention studies assessing the effectiveness of ACE inhibitors or angiotensin II receptor antagonists in delaying progression to overt nephropathy in adolescents with microalbuminuria. Therefore, treatment of adolescents with persistent microalbuminuria is based on the effectiveness of treatments in adults with type 1 diabetes (115).

Retinopathy

Retinopathy is rare in prepubertal children with type 1 diabetes and in postpubertal adolescents with good metabolic control (116,117).

Neuropathy

When present, neuropathy is mostly subclinical in children (118). While prospective nerve conduction studies and autonomic neuropathy assessment studies have demonstrated increased prevalence of abnormalities over time (119), persistence of abnormalities is an inconsistent finding (120). Vibration and monofilament testing have suboptimal sensitivity and specificity in adolescents (121). With the exception of intensifying diabetes management to achieve and maintain glycemic targets, no other treatment modality has been studied in children and adolescents.

Dyslipidemia

Most children with type 1 diabetes should be considered at low risk for vascular disease associated with dyslipidemia (122,123). The exceptions are those with longer duration of disease, microvascular complications or other cardiovascular disease (CVD) risk factors, including smoking, hypertension, obesity and/or family history of premature CVD (124). Dyslipidemia screening should be targeted at those >12 years of age and younger children with specific risk factors for dyslipidemia. Statin therapy has only rarely been studied specifically in children with diabetes, and there is no evidence linking specific low-density lipoprotein cholesterol (LDL-C) cutoffs in children with diabetes with long-term outcomes. In pubertal children without diabetes but with familial hypercholesterolemia, statin therapy is safe and effective at lowering LDL-C levels and attenuating progression of surrogate markers for future vascular disease (125).

Hypertension

Up to 16% of adolescents with type 1 diabetes have hypertension (126). Twenty-four-hour ambulatory blood pressure (BP) monitoring has been used to exclude white coat hypertension and to identify loss of diurnal systolic rhythm (nondippers) with nocturnal hypertension in some normotensive adolescents with type 1

diabetes (127). These abnormalities may be predictive of future microalbuminuria (127). However, the role of ambulatory BP monitoring in routine care remains uncertain. Children with type 1 diabetes and confirmed hypertension should be treated according to the guidelines for children without diabetes (128).

Transition to Adult Care

The change of physician or DHC team can have a major impact on disease management and metabolic control in the person with diabetes (129). Between 25% and 65% of young adults have no medical follow-up during the transition from pediatric to adult diabetes care services (130,131). Those with no follow-up are more likely to experience hospitalization for DKA during this period. Organized transition services may decrease the rate of loss of follow-up (132,133).

RECOMMENDATIONS

Delivery of care

1. All children with diabetes should have access to an experienced pediatric DHC team and specialized care starting at diagnosis [Grade D, Level 4 (1)].

2. Children with new-onset type 1 diabetes who are medically stable should receive their initial education and management in an outpatient setting, provided that appropriate personnel and daily communication with the DHC are available [Grade B, Level 1A (3)].

3. To ensure ongoing and adequate diabetes care, adolescents should receive care from a specialized program aimed at creating a well-prepared and supported transition to adult care that includes a transition coordinator, patient reminders, and support and education, with or without a joint pediatric and adult clinic [Grade C, Level 3 (132,133)].

Glycemic targets

4. Glycemic targets should be graduated with age (see Table 1):
   - Children <6 years of age should aim for an A1C <8.0% [Grade D, Consensus]. Caution should be used to minimize hypoglycemia because of the potential association in this age group between severe hypoglycemia and later cognitive impairment [Grade D, Level 4 (134)].
   - Children 6–12 years of age should aim for a target A1C ≤7.5% [Grade D, Consensus].
   - Adolescents should aim for the same glycemic targets as adults [Grade A, Level 1A (5)].

5. Children with persistently poor glycemic control (e.g. A1C >10%) should be assessed by a specialized pediatric diabetes team for a comprehensive interdisciplinary assessment and referred for psychosocial support as indicated [Grade D, Consensus]. Intensive family and individualized psychological interventions aimed at improving glycemic control should be considered to improve chronically poor metabolic control [Grade A, Level 1A (34,35,135)].

Insulin therapy

6. Children with new-onset diabetes should be started on at least 2 daily injections of bolus insulin (e.g. short-acting bolus insulin or rapid-acting bolus insulin analogues) combined with basal insulin (e.g. intermediate-acting insulin or long-acting basal insulin analogue) [Grade D, Consensus].

7. Insulin therapy should be assessed at each clinical encounter to ensure it still enables the child to meet A1C targets, minimizes the risk of hypoglycemia and allows flexibility in carbohydrate intake, daily schedule and activities [Grade D, Consensus]. If these goals are not being met, an intensified diabetes management approach (including increased education, monitoring and contact with diabetes team) should be used [Grade A, Level 1(4) for adolescents; Grade D, Consensus for younger children], and treatment options may include the following:
   - Increased frequency of injections [Grade D, Consensus].
   - Change in the type of basal and/or bolus insulin [Grade B, Level 2 (19), for adolescents; Grade D, Consensus, for younger children].
   - Change to continuous subcutaneous insulin infusion therapy [Grade C, Level 3 (136)].

Hypoglycemia

8. In children, the use of mini-doses of glucagon (10 μg per year of age with minimum dose 20 μg and maximum dose 150 μg) should be considered in the home management of mild or impending hypoglycemia associated with inability or refusal to take oral carbohydrate [Grade D, Level 4 (32)].

9. In the home situation, severe hypoglycemia in an unconscious child >5 years of age should be treated with 1 mg glucagon subcutaneously or intramuscularly. In children ≤5 years of age, a dose of 0.5 mg glucagon should be given. The episode should be discussed with the diabetes healthcare team as soon as possible and consideration given to reducing insulin doses for the next 24 hours to prevent further severe hypoglycemia [Grade D, Consensus].

10. Dextrose 0.5–1 g/kg should be given over 1–3 minutes to treat severe hypoglycemia with unconsciousness when IV access is available [Grade D, Consensus].

Diabetic ketoacidosis (DKA)

11. To prevent DKA in children with diabetes:
    - Targeted public awareness campaigns should be considered to educate parents and other caregivers (e.g. teachers) about the early symptoms of diabetes [Grade C, Level 3 (42)].
    - Comprehensive education and support services [Grade C, Level 3 (43)], as well as 24-hour telephone services [Grade C, Level 3 (44)], should be available for families of children with diabetes.

12. DKA in children should be treated according to pediatric-specific protocols [Grade D, Consensus]. If appropriate expertise/facilities are not available locally, there should be immediate consultation with a centre with expertise in pediatric diabetes [Grade D, Consensus].

13. In children in DKA, rapid administration of hypotonic fluids should be avoided [Grade D, Level 4 (49)]. Circulatory compromise should be treated with only enough isotonic fluids to correct circulatory inadequacy [Grade D, Consensus]. Restoration of extracellular fluid volume should be extended over a 48-hour period with regular reassessments of fluid deficits [Grade D, Level 4 (49)].

14. In children in DKA, IV insulin bolus should not be given; an IV infusion of short-acting insulin should be used at an initial dose of 0.1 units/kg/h [Grade D, Level 4 (53)]. The insulin infusion should not be started until 1 hour after starting fluid replacement therapy [Grade D, Level 4 (52)].

15. In children in DKA, the insulin infusion rate should be maintained until the plasma anion gap normalizes. Once plasma glucose reaches 14.0–17.0 mmol/L, IV glucose should be started to prevent hypoglycemia [Grade D, Consensus].

16. In children in DKA, administration of sodium bicarbonate should be avoided except in extreme circulatory compromise, as this may contribute to cerebral edema [Grade D, Level 4 (48)].

Microvascular complications

17. Screening for microalbuminuria should be performed annually, commencing at 12 years of age in children with type 1 diabetes >5 years' duration [Grade D, Consensus].

18. Children ≥12 years should be screened for microalbuminuria with a first morning urine ACR (preferred) [Grade B, Level 2 (111)] or a random ACR [Grade D, Consensus]. Abnormal results should be confirmed [Grade B, Level 2 (137)] at least 1 month later with a first morning ACR or timed, overnight urine collection for albumin excretion rate [Grade D, Consensus]. Microalbuminuria (ACR >2.5 mg/mmol) should not be diagnosed in children ≥12 years unless it is persistent, as demonstrated by 2 consecutive first morning ACR or timed collections obtained at 3- to 4-month intervals over a 6- to 12-month period [Grade D, Consensus].

19. Children ≥12 years with persistent microalbuminuria should be treated per adult guidelines (see Chronic Kidney Disease chapter, p. S129) [Grade D, Consensus].

20. In children ≥15 years of age with type 1 diabetes, screening and evaluation for retinopathy by an expert professional should be performed annually, starting 5 years after the onset of diabetes [Grade D, Consensus]. The screening interval can be increased to every 2 years in children with type 1 diabetes who have good glycemic control, duration of diabetes <10 years and no significant retinopathy (as determined by an expert professional) [Grade D, Consensus].

21. Postpubertal children with type 1 diabetes of >5 years' duration and poor metabolic control should be questioned about symptoms of numbness, pain, cramps and paresthesia, and examined for skin sensation, vibration sense, light touch and ankle reflexes [Grade D, Consensus].

Comorbid conditions and other complications

22. Children and adolescents with diabetes, along with their families, should be screened regularly for psychosocial or psychological disorders [Grade D, Level 4 (108,109)] and should be referred to an expert in mental health and/or psychosocial issues for intervention when required (Grade D, Consensus).

23. Adolescent females with type 1 diabetes should be regularly screened using nonjudgemental questions about weight and body image concerns, dieting, binge eating and insulin omission for weight loss [Grade D, Consensus].

24. Children with type 1 diabetes who are <12 years of age should be screened for dyslipidemia if they have other risk factors, such as obesity (body mass index >95th percentile for age and gender) and/or a family history of dyslipidemia or premature cardiovascular disease. Routine screening for dyslipidemia should begin at 12 years of age, with repeat screening after 5 years [Grade D, Consensus].

25. Once dyslipidemia is diagnosed in children with type 1 diabetes, the dyslipidemia should be treated per lipid guidelines for adults with diabetes [Grade D, Consensus].

26. All children with type 1 diabetes should be screened for hypertension at least twice annually [Grade D, Consensus].

27. Children with type 1 diabetes and BP readings persistently above the 95th percentile for age should receive lifestyle counselling, including weight loss if overweight [Grade D, Level 4 (138)]. If BP remains elevated, treatment should be initiated based on recommendations for children without diabetes [Grade D, Consensus].

28. Influenza immunization should be offered to children with diabetes as a way to prevent an intercurrent illness that could complicate diabetes management [Grade D, Consensus].

29. Formal smoking prevention and cessation counselling should be part of diabetes management for children with diabetes [Grade D, Consensus].

30. Adolescent females with type 1 diabetes should receive counselling on contraception and sexual health in order to prevent unplanned pregnancy [Grade D, Level 4 (139)].

31. Children with type 1 diabetes who have thyroid antibodies should be considered high risk for autoimmune thyroid disease [Grade C, Level 3 (100)]. Children with type 1 diabetes should be screened at diabetes diagnosis with repeat screening every 2 years using a serum thyroid-stimulating hormone and thyroid peroxidase antibodies [Grade D, Consensus]. More frequent screening is indicated in the presence of positive thyroid antibodies, thyroid symptoms or goiter [Grade D, Consensus].

32. Children with type 1 diabetes and symptoms of classic or atypical celiac disease (see Table 4) should undergo celiac screening [Grade D, Consensus] and, if confirmed, be treated with a gluten-free diet to improve symptoms [Grade D, Level 4 (104)] and prevent the long-term sequelae of untreated classic celiac disease [Grade D, Level 4 (105)]. Parents should be informed that the need for screening and treatment of asymptomatic (silent) celiac disease is controversial [Grade D, Consensus].

Abbreviations:
A1C, glycated hemoglobin; *ACR*, albumin to creatinine ratio; *BP*, blood pressure; *DHC*, diabetes healthcare; *IV*, intravenous.

References

1. Glasgow AM, Weissberg-Benchell J, Tynan WD, et al. Readmissions of children with diabetes mellitus to a children's hospital. Pediatrics 1991;88:98–104.
2. von SS, Muller-Godeffroy E, Hager S, et al. Mobile diabetes education and care: intervention for children and young people with Type 1 diabetes in rural areas of northern Germany. Diabet Med 2006;23:122–7.
3. Clar C, Waugh N, Thomas S. Routine hospital admission versus out-patient or home care in children at diagnosis of type 1 diabetes mellitus. Cochrane Database Syst Rev 2006;2:CD004099.

4. The Diabetes Control and Complications Trial Research Group. Effect of intensive treatment of diabetes on the development and progression of long-term complications in insulin-dependent diabetes mellitus. N Engl J Med 1993;329:977–86.
5. The Diabetes Control and Complications Trial Research Group. Effect of intensive diabetes treatment on the development and progression of long-term complications in adolescents with insulin-dependent diabetes mellitus: Diabetes Control and Complications Trial. J Pediatr 1994;125:177–88.
6. Gaudieri PA, Chen R, Greer TF, Holmes CS. Cognitive function in children with type 1 diabetes: a meta-analysis. Diabetes Care 2008;31:1892–7.
7. Schoenle EJ, Schoenle D, Molinari L, et al. Impaired intellectual development in children with Type I diabetes: association with HbA(1c), age at diagnosis and sex. Diabetologia 2002;45:108–14.
8. Ferguson SC, Blane A, Wardlaw J, et al. Influence of an early-onset age of type 1 diabetes on cerebral structure and cognitive function. Diabetes Care 2005; 28:1431–7.
9. Strudwick SK, Carne C, Gardiner J, et al. Cognitive functioning in children with early onset type 1 diabetes and severe hypoglycemia. J Pediatr 2005;147: 680–5.
10. Asvold BO, Sand T, Hestad K, Bjorgaas MR. Cognitive function in type 1 diabetic adults with early exposure to severe hypoglycemia: a 16-year follow-up study. Diabetes Care 2010 Sep;33:1945–7.
11. Swift PG, Skinner TC, de Beaufort CE, et al, Hvidoere Study Group on Childhood Diabetes. Target setting in intensive insulin management is associated with metabolic control: the Hvidoere childhood diabetes study group centre differences study 2005. Pediatr Diabetes 2010;11:271–8.
12. Robertson KJ, Schoenle E, Gucev Z, et al. Insulin detemir compared with NPH insulin in children and adolescents with Type 1 diabetes. Diabet Med 2007; 24:27–34.
13. Chase HP, Arslanian S, White NH, Tamborlane WV. Insulin glargine versus intermediate-acting insulin as the basal component of multiple daily injection regimens for adolescents with type 1 diabetes mellitus. J Pediatr 2008;153: 547–53.
14. Phillip M, Battelino T, Rodriguez H, et al. Use of insulin pump therapy in the pediatric age-group. Consensus statement from the European Society for Paediatric Endocrinology, the Lawson Wilkins Pediatric Endocrine Society, and the International Society for Pediatric and Adolescent Diabetes, endorsed by the American Diabetes Association and the European Association for the Study of Diabetes. Diabetes Care 2007;30:1653–62.
15. Misso ML, Egberts KJ, Page M, et al. Subcutaneous insulin infusion (CSII) versus multiple insulin injections for type 1 diabetes mellitus. Cochrane Database Syst Rev 2010;1:CD005103.
16. Weinzimer SA, Sikes KA, Steffen AT, et al. Insulin pump treatment of childhood type 1 diabetes. Pediatr Clin North Am 2005;52:1677–88.
17. Bergenstal RM, Tamborlane WV, Ahmann A, et al. Effectiveness of sensor-augmented insulin-pump therapy in type 1 diabetes. N Engl J Med 2010; 363:311–20.
18. Alemzadeh R, Berhe T, Wyatt DT. Flexible insulin therapy with glargine insulin improved glycemic control and reduced severe hypoglycemia among preschool-aged children with type 1 diabetes mellitus. Pediatrics 2005;115: 1320–4.
19. Murphy NP, Keane SM, Ong KK, et al. Randomized cross-over trial of insulin glargine plus lispro or NPH insulin plus regular human insulin in adolescents with type 1 diabetes on intensive insulin regimens. Diabetes Care 2003;26: 799–804.
20. Hassan K, Rodriguez LM, Johnson SE, et al. A randomized, controlled trial comparing twice-a-day insulin glargine mixed with rapid-acting insulin analogs versus standard neutral protamine Hagedorn (NPH) therapy in newly diagnosed type 1 diabetes. Pediatrics 2008;121:e466–72.
21. de Beaufort CE, Swift PG, Skinner CT, et al, Hvidoere Study Group on Childhood Diabetes 2005. Continuing stability of center differences in pediatric diabetes care: do advances in diabetes treatment improve outcome? Diabetes Care 2007;30:2245–50.
22. Rosenbauer J, Dost A, Karges B, et al, the DPV Initiative and the German BMBF Competence Network Diabetes Mellitus. Improved metabolic control in children and adolescents with type 1 diabetes: a trend analysis using prospective multicenter data from Germany and Austria. Diabetes Care 2012; 35:80–6.
23. Nordly S, Mortensen HB, Andreasen AH, et al. Factors associated with glycaemic outcome of childhood diabetes care in Denmark. Diabet Med 2005;22: 1566–73.
24. Tamborlane WV, Beck RW, Bode BW, et al, Juvenile Diabetes Research Foundation Continuous Glucose Monitoring Study Group. Continuous glucose monitoring and intensive treatment of type 1 diabetes. N Engl J Med 2008; 359:1464–76.
25. Health Canada. Eating Well with Canada's Food Guide. Ottawa, ON: Health Canada, Health Products and Food Branch, Office of Nutrition Policy and Promotion; 2007. Publication H39–166/1990E.
26. Patton SR, Dolan LM, Powers SW. Dietary adherence and associated glycemic control in families of young children with type 1 diabetes. J Am Diet Assoc 2007;107:46–52.
27. Mehta SN, Quinn N, Volkening LK, Laffel LMB. Impact of carbohydrate counting on glycemic control in children with type 1 diabetes. Diabetes Care 2009;32:1014–6.
28. Markowitz JT, Butler DA, Volkening LK, et al. Brief screening tool for disordered eating in diabetes internal consistency and external validity in a contemporary sample of pediatric patients with type 1 diabetes. Diabetes Care 2010;33:495–500.
29. Naguib JM, Kulinskaya E, Lomax CL, Garralda ME. Neuro-cognitive performance in children with type 1 diabetes: a meta-analysis. J Pediatr Psychol 2009;34:271–82.
30. Garg S, Moser E, Dain MP, Rodionova A. Clinical experience with insulin glargine in type 1 diabetes. Diabetes Technol Ther 2010;12:835–46.
31. Juvenile Diabetes Research Foundation Continuous Glucose Monitoring Study Group. Effectiveness of continuous glucose monitoring in a clinical care environment. Evidence from the Juvenile Diabetes Research Foundation Continuous Glucose Monitoring (JDRF-CGM) trial. Diabetes Care 2010;33: 17–22.
32. Hartley M, Thomsett MJ, Cotterill AM. Mini-dose glucagon rescue for mild hypoglycaemia in children with type 1 diabetes: the Brisbane experience. J Paediatr Child Health 2006;42:108–11.
33. Haymond MW, Schreiner B. Mini-dose glucagon rescue for hypoglycemia in children with type 1 diabetes. Diabetes Care 2001;24:643–5.
34. Winkley K, Ismail K, Landau S, et al. Psychological interventions to improve glycaemic control in patients with type 1 diabetes: systematic review and meta-analysis of randomised controlled trials. BMJ 2006;333:65.
35. Hood KK, Rohan JM, Peterson CM, Drotar D. Interventions with adherence-promoting components in pediatric type 1 diabetes: meta-analysis of their impact on glycemic control. Diabetes Care 2010;33:1658–64.
36. Levy-Marchal C, Patterson CC, Green A. Geographic variation of presentation at diagnosis of type 1 diabetes in children: the EURODIAB study. Diabetologia 2001;44(suppl 3):B75–80.
37. Patterson CC, Dahlquist G, Harjutsalo V, et al. Early mortality in EURODIAB population-based cohorts of type 1 diabetes diagnosed in childhood since 1989. Diabetologia 2007;50:2439–42.
38. Vanelli M, Chiari G, Ghizzoni L, et al. Effectiveness of a prevention program for diabetic ketoacidosis in children: an 8-year study in schools and private practices. Diabetes Care 1999;22:7–9.
39. Keenan HT, Foster CM, Bratton SL. Social factors associated with prolonged hospitalization among diabetic children. Pediatrics 2002;109:40–4.
40. Hanas R, Lindgren F, Lindblad B. A 2-yr national population study of pediatric ketoacidosis in Sweden: predisposing conditions and insulin pump use. Pediatr Diabetes 2009;10:33–7.
41. Karges B, Kapellen T, Neu A, et al, Diabetes Prospective Documentation DPV Initiative, German Federal Ministry for Education and Research BMBF Competence Network of Diabetes Mellitus. Long-acting insulin analogs and the risk of diabetic ketoacidosis in children and adolescents with type 1 diabetes: a prospective study of 10,682 patients from 271 institutions. Diabetes Care 2010;33:1031–3.
42. Drozda DJ, Dawson VA, Long DJ, et al. Assessment of the effect of a comprehensive diabetes management program on hospital admission rates of children with diabetes mellitus. Diabetes Educ 1990;16:389–93.
43. Ellis D, Naar-King S, Templin T, et al. Multisystemic therapy for adolescents with poorly controlled type 1 diabetes: reduced diabetic ketoacidosis admissions and related costs over 24 months. Diabetes Care 2008;31: 1746–67.
44. Hoffman WH, O'Neill P, Khoury C, et al. Service and education for the insulin-dependent child. Diabetes Care 1978;1:285–8.
45. Chiari G, Ghidini B, Vanelli M. Effectiveness of a toll-free telephone hotline for children and adolescents with type 1 diabetes. A 5-year study. Acta Biomed 2003;74(suppl 1):45–8.
46. Edge JA, Hawkins MM, Winter DL, et al. The risk and outcome of cerebral oedema developing during diabetic ketoacidosis. Arch Dis Child 2001;85: 16–22.
47. Rosenbloom AL. Intracerebral crises during treatment of diabetic ketoacidosis. Diabetes Care 1990;13:22–33.
48. Glaser N, Barnett P, McCaslin I, et al. Risk factors for cerebral edema in children with diabetic ketoacidosis. N Engl J Med 2001;344:264–9.
49. Harris GD, Fiordalisi I, Harris WL, et al. Minimizing the risk of brain herniation during treatment of diabetic ketoacidemia: a retrospective and prospective study. J Pediatr 1990;117:22–31.
50. Harris GD, Fiordalisi I. Physiologic management of diabetic ketoacidemia. A 5-year prospective pediatric experience in 231 episodes. Arch Pediatr Adolesc Med 1994;148:1046–52.
51. Hale PM, Rezvani I, Braunstein AW, et al. Factors predicting cerebral edema in young children with diabetic ketoacidosis and new onset type I diabetes. Acta Paediatr 1997;86.626–31.
52. Edge JA, Jakes RW, Roy Y, et al. The UK case-control study of cerebral oedema complicating diabetic ketoacidosis in children. Diabetologia 2006;49:2002–9.
53. Fort P, Waters SM, Lifshitz F. Low-dose insulin infusion in the treatment of diabetic ketoacidosis: bolus versus no bolus. J Pediatr 1980;96:36–40.
54. Lindsay R, Bolte RG. The use of an insulin bolus in low-dose insulin infusion for pediatric diabetic ketoacidosis. Pediatr Emerg Care 1989;5:77–9.
55. Hoorn EJ, Carlotti AP, Costa LA, et al. Preventing a drop in effective plasma osmolality to minimize the likelihood of cerebral edema during treatment of children with diabetic ketoacidosis. J Pediatr 2007;150:467–73.
56. Muir AB, Quisling RG, Yang MC, et al. Cerebral edema in childhood diabetic ketoacidosis: natural history, radiographic findings, and early identification. Diabetes Care 2004;27:1541–6.
57. Wolfsdorf J, Craig ME, Daneman D, et al, International Society for Pediatric and Adolescent Diabetes. Diabetic ketoacidosis. Pediatr Diabetes 2007;8: 28–43.

58. National Advisory Committee on Immunization. Canadian Immunization Guide. 7th ed. Ottawa, ON: Public Health Agency of Canada; 2006.
59. Infectious Diseases and Immunization Committee, Canadian Paediatric Society. Pneumococcal vaccine for children. Paediatr Child Health 2002;6:214–7.
60. Infectious Diseases and Immunization Committee, Canadian Paediatric Society. Recommendations for the use of influenza vaccine for children. Paediatr Child Health 2004;9:283–4.
61. Davies P, Nwokoro C, Leigh M. Vaccinations against influenza and pneumococcus in children with diabetes: telephone questionnaire survey. BMJ 2004;328:203.
62. Irwin DE, Weatherby LB, Huang WY, et al. Impact of patient characteristics on the risk of influenza/ILI-related complications. BMC Health Serv Res 2001;1:8.
63. Zuccotti GV, Scaramuzza A, Riboni S, et al. Long-lasting immunogenicity of a virosomal vaccine in older children and young adults with type 1 diabetes mellitus. Vaccine 2009;27:5357–62.
64. Scott LJ, Warram JH, Hanna LS, et al. A nonlinear effect of hyperglycemia and current cigarette smoking are major determinants of the onset of microalbuminuria in type 1 diabetes. Diabetes 2001;50:2842–9.
65. Hofer SE, Rosenbauer J, Grulich-Henn J, et al, DPV-Wiss Study Group. Smoking and metabolic control in adolescents with type 1 diabetes. J Pediatr 2009;154:20–3.
66. Carmody D, Doyle A, Firth RGR, et al. Teenage pregnancy in type 1 diabetes mellitus. Pediatr Diabetes 2010;11:111–5.
67. Fogel NR, Weissberg-Benchell J. Preventing poor psychological and health outcomes in pediatric type 1 diabetes. Current Diab Rep 2010;10:436–43.
68. Lawrence JM, Standiford DA, Loots B, et al. Prevalence and correlates of depressed mood among youth with diabetes: The SEARCH for Diabetes in Youth Study. Pediatrics 2006;117:1348–58.
69. Hood KK, Huestis S, Maher A, et al. Depressive symptoms in children and adolescents with type 1 diabetes. Diabetes Care 2006;29:1389–91.
70. Northam EA, Matthews LK, Anderson PJ, et al. Psychiatric morbidity and health outcome in Type 1 diabetes: perspectives from a prospective longitudinal study. Diabet Med 2005;22:152–7.
71. Kakleas K, Kandyla B, Karayianni C, Karavanaki K. Psychosocial problems in adolescents with type 1 diabetes mellitus. Diabetes Metab 2009;35:339–50.
72. McDonnell DM, Northam EA, Donath SM, et al. Hyperglycemia and externalizing behavior in children with type 1 diabetes. Diabetes Care 2007;30:2211–5.
73. Korbel DC, Wiebe DJ, Berg CA, Palmer DL. Gender differences in adherence to type 1 diabetes management across adolescence: the medicating role of depression. Children's Healthcare 2007;36:83–98.
74. Bryden KS, Neil A, Mayou RA, et al. Eating habits, body weight, and insulin misuse: a longitudinal study of teenagers and young adults with type 1 diabetes. Diabetes Care 1999;22:1956–60.
75. Herzer M, Hood KK. Anxiety symptoms in adolescents with type 1 diabetes: association with blood glucose monitoring and glycemic control. J Pediatr Psychol 2009;35:415–25.
76. Chida Y, Hamer M. An association of adverse psychosocial factors with diabetes mellitus: a meta-analytic review of longitudinal cohort studies. Diabetologia 2008;51:2168–78.
77. Gonzalez JS, Peyrot M, McCarl LA, et al. Depression and diabetes treatment nonadherence: a meta-analysis. Diabetes Care 2008;31:2398–403.
78. Stewart SWM, Rao U, Emslie GJ, et al. Depressive symptoms predict hospitalization for adolescents with type 1 diabetes mellitus. Pediatrics 2005;115:1315–9.
79. Garrison MM, Katon WJ, Richardson LP. The impact of psychiatric comorbidities on readmissions for diabetes in youth. Diabetes Care 2005;28:2150–4.
80. Hassan K, Loar R, Anderson BJ, Heptulla RA. The role of socioeconomic status, depression, quality of life, and glycemic control in type 1 diabetes mellitus. J Pediatr 2006;149:526–31.
81. Hood KK. The influence of caregiver depressive symptoms on proxy report of youth depressive symptoms: a test of the depression-distortion hypothesis in pediatric type 1 diabetes. J Pediatr Psychol 2009;34:294–303.
82. Cunningham NR, Vesco AT, Dolan LM, Hood KK. From caregiver psychological distress to adolescent glycemic control: the mediating role of perceived burden around diabetes management. J Pediatc Psychol 2011;36:196–295.
83. Butler JM, Skinner M, Gelfand D, et al. Maternal parenting style and adjustment in adolescents with type 1 diabetes. J Pediatr Psychol 2007;32:1227–37.
84. Jaser SS, Whittemore R, Ambrosino JM, et al. Mediators of depressive symptoms in children with type 1 diabetes and their mothers. J Pediatr Psychol 2008;33:509–19.
85. Eckshtain D, Ellis DA, Kolmodin K, Naar-King S. The effects of parental depression and parenting practices on depressive symptoms and metabolic control in urban youth with insulin dependent diabetes. J Pediatr Psychol 2010;35:426–35.
86. Cameron LD, Young MJ, Wiebe DJ. Maternal trait anxiety and diabetes control in adolescents with type 1 diabetes. J Pediatr Psychol 2007;32:733–44.
87. Jones JM, Lawson ML, Daneman D, et al. Eating disorders in adolescent females with and without type 1 diabetes: cross sectional study. BMJ 2000;320:1563–6.
88. Rydall AC, Rodin GM, Olmsted MP, et al. Disordered eating behavior and microvascular complications in young women with insulin-dependent diabetes mellitus. N Engl J Med 1997;336:1849–54.

89. Young-Hyman DL, Davis CL. Disordered eating behavior in individuals with diabetes. importance of context, evaluation, and classification. Diabetes Care 2010;33:683–9.
90. Schwartz DD, Cline VD, Hansen JA, et al. Early risk factors for nonadherence in pediatric type 1 diabetes: a review of the recent literature. Curr Diabetes Rev 2010;6:167–83.
91. Cameron FJ, Northam EA, Ambler GR, Daneman D. Routine psychological screening in youth with type 1 diabetes and their parents. Diabetes Care 2007;30:2716–24.
92. Harkness E, MacDonald W, Valderas J, et al. Identifying psychosocial interventions that improve both physical and mental health in patients with diabetes. Diabetes Care 2010;33:926–30.
93. De Wit M, Dellemarre-Van De Waal HA, Bokma JA, et al. Monitoring and discussing health-related quality of life in adolescents with type 1 diabetes improve psychosocial well-being. Diabetes Care 2008;31:1521–6.
94. Van der Feltz-Cornelis CM, Nuyen J, Stoop C, et al. Effective of interventions for major depressive disorder and significant depressive symptoms in patients with diabetes mellitus: a systematic review and meta-analysis. Gen Hosp Psychiatry 2010;32:380–95.
95. Rossello JM, Jimenez-Chafety MI. Cognitive-behavioral group therapy for depression in adolescents with diabetes: a pilot study. Interam J Psychol 2006;40:219–26.
96. Alam R, Sturt J, Lall R, Winkley K. An updated meta-analysis to assess the effectiveness of psychological interventions delivered by psychological specialists and generalist clinicians on glycaemic control and on psychological status. Patient Educ Couns 2009;75:25–36.
97. Delamater AM, Jacobson AM, Anderson B, et al. Psychosocial therapies in diabetes: report of the Psychosocial Therapies Working Group. Diabetes Care 2001;24:1286–92.
98. Mendez FJ, Belendez M. Effects of a behavioral intervention on treatment adherence and stress management in adolescents with IDDM. Diabetes Care 1997;20:1370–5.
99. Barker JM. Clinical review: type 1 diabetes-associated autoimmunity: natural history, genetic associations, and screening. J Clin Endocrinol Metab 2006;91:1210–7.
100. Glastras SJ, Craig ME, Verge CF, et al. The role of autoimmunity at diagnosis of type 1 diabetes in the development of thyroid and celiac disease and microvascular complications. Diabetes Care 2005;28:2170–5.
101. Kordonouri O, Hartmann R, Deiss D, et al. Natural course of autoimmune thyroiditis in type 1 diabetes: association with gender, age, diabetes duration, and puberty. Arch Dis Child 2005;90:411–4.
102. Marks SD, Girgis R, Couch RM. Screening for adrenal antibodies in children with type 1 diabetes and autoimmune thyroid disease. Diabetes Care 2003;26:3187–8.
103. Cerutti F, Bruno G, Chiarelli F, et al. Younger age at onset and sex predict celiac disease in children and adolescents with type 1 diabetes: an Italian multicenter study. Diabetes Care 2004;27:1294–8.
104. Mayer M, Greco L, Troncone R, et al. Compliance of adolescents with celiac disease with a gluten-free diet. Gut 1991;32:881–5.
105. Holmes GK, Prior P, Lane MR, et al. Malignancy in coeliac disease: effect of a gluten free diet. Gut 1989;30:333–8.
106. Lang-Muritano M, Molinari L, Dommann-Scherrer C, et al. Incidence of enteropathy-associated T-cell lymphoma in celiac disease: implications for children and adolescents with type 1 diabetes. Pediatr Diabetes 2002;3:42–5.
107. Rami B, Sumnik Z, Schober E, et al. Screening detected celiac disease in children with type 1 diabetes mellitus: effect on the clinical course (a case control study). J Pediatr Gastroenterol Nutr 2005;41:317–21.
108. Donaghue KC, Craig ME, Chan AK. Prevalence of diabetes complications 6 years after diagnosis in an incident cohort of childhood diabetes. Diabet Med 2005;22:711–8.
109. Schultz CJ, Konopelska-Bahu T, Dalton RN, et al. Microalbuminuria prevalence varies with age, sex, and puberty in children with type 1 diabetes followed from diagnosis in a longitudinal study. Oxford Regional Prospective Study Group. Diabetes Care 1999;22:495–502.
110. Gatling W, Knight C, Hill RD. Screening for early diabetic nephropathy: which sample to detect microalbuminuria? Diabet Med 1985;2:451–5.
111. Shield JP, Hunt LP, Baum JD, et al. Screening for diabetic microalbuminuria in routine clinical care: which method? Arch Dis Child 1995;72:524–5.
112. Hogg RI, Furth S, Lemley KV, et al. National Kidney Foundation's Kidney Disease Outcomes Quality Initiative. Clinical Practice Guidelines for Chronic Kidney Disease in Children and Adolescents: Evaluation, Classification, and Stratification. Pediatrics 2003;111:1416–21.
113. Stone ML, Craig ME, Chan AK, et al. Natural history and risk factors for microalbuminuria in adolescents with type 1 diabetes: a longitudinal study. Diabetes Care 2006;29:2072–7.
114. Cook J, Daneman D, Spino M, et al. Angiotensin converting enzyme inhibitor therapy to decrease microalbuminuria in normotensive children with insulin-dependent diabetes mellitus. J Pediatr 1990;117:39–45.
115. ACE Inhibitors in Diabetic Nephropathy Trialist Group. Should all patients with type 1 diabetes mellitus and microalbuminuria receive angiotensin-converting enzyme inhibitors? A meta-analysis of individual patient data. Ann Intern Med 2001;134:370–9.
116. Maguire A, Chan A, Cusumano J, et al. The case for biennial retinopathy screening in children and adolescents. Diabetes Care 2005;28:509–13.

73

117. Huo B, Steffen AT, Swan K, et al. Clinical outcomes and cost-effectiveness of retinopathy screening in youth with type 1 diabetes. Diabetes Care 2007;30: 362–3.
118. Karavanaki K, Baum JD. Coexistence of impaired indices of autonomic neuropathy and diabetic nephropathy in a cohort of children with type 1 diabetes mellitus. J Pediatr Endocrinol Metab 2003;16:79–90.
119. Olsen BS, Sjølie A-K, Hougaard P, et al. A 6-year nationwide cohort study of glycaemic control in young people with type 1 diabetes. Risk markers for the development of retinopathy, nephropathy, and neuropathy. J Diabetes Complications 2000;14:295–300.
120. Donaghue KC, Fung ATW, Fairchild JM, et al. Prospective assessment of autonomic and peripheral nerve function in adolescents with diabetes. Diabet Med 1996;13:65–71.
121. Nelson D, Mah JK, Adams C, et al. Comparison of conventional and non-invasive techniques for the early identification of diabetic neuropathy in children and adolescents with type 1 diabetes. Pediatr Diabetes 2006;7:305–10.
122. Schwab KO, Doerfer J, Marg W, et al, DPV Science Initiative and the Competence Network Diabetes mellitus. Characterization of 33 488 children and adolescents with type 1 diabetes based on the gender-specific increase of cardiovascular risk factors. Pediatr Diabetes 2010;11:357–63.
123. Margeirsdottir HD, Larsen JR, Brunborg C, et al, Norwegian Study Group for Childhood Diabetes. High prevalence of cardiovascular risk factors in children and adolescents with type 1 diabetes: a population-based study. Diabetologia 2008;51:554–61.
124. Celermajer DS, Ayer JGJ. Childhood risk factors for adult cardiovascular disease and primary prevention in childhood. Heart 2006;92:1701–6.
125. Vuorio A, Kuoppala J, Kovanen PT, et al. Statins for children with familial hypercholesterolemia. Cochrane Database Syst Rev 2010;7:CD006401.
126. Eppens MC, Craig ME, Cusumano J, et al. Prevalence of diabetes complications in adolescents with type 2 compared with type 1 diabetes. Diabetes Care 2006;29:1300–6.
127. Lurbe E, Redon J, Kesani A, et al. Increase in nocturnal blood pressure and progression to microalbuminuria in type 1 diabetes. N Engl J Med 2002;347: 797–805.
128. National Heart, Lung and Blood Institute. Blood Pressure Tables for Children and Adolescents from the Fourth Report on the Diagnosis, Evaluation, and Treatment of High Blood Pressure in Children and Adolescents. 2004. Available at: http://www.nhlbi.nih.gov/guidelines/hypertension/child_tbl.pdf. Accessed June 24, 2011.
129. Nakhla M, Daneman D, To T, et al. Transition to adult care for youths with diabetes mellitus: findings from a Universal Health Care System. Pediatrics 2009;124:e1134–41.
130. Frank M. Factors associated with non-compliance with a medical follow-up regimen after discharge from a pediatric diabetes clinic. Can J Diabetes 1996;20:13–20.
131. Pacaud D, Yale JF, Stephure D, et al. Problems in transition from pediatric care to adult care for individuals with diabetes. Can J Diabetes 2005;29: 13–8.
132. Van Walleghem N, Macdonald CA, Dean HJ. Evaluation of a systems navigator model for transition from pediatric to adult care for young adults with type 1 diabetes. Diabetes Care 2008;31:1529–30.
133. Holmes-Walker DJ, Llewellyn AC, Farrell K. A transition care programme which improves diabetes control and reduces hospital admission rates in young adults with Type 1 diabetes aged 15-25 years. Diabet Med 2007;24: 764–9.
134. Hershey T, Perantie DC, Warren SL, et al. Frequency and timing of severe hypoglycemia affects spatial memory in children with type 1 diabetes. Diabetes Care 2005;28:2372–7.
135. Armour TA, Norris SL, Jack Jr L, et al. The effectiveness of family interventions in people with diabetes mellitus: a systematic review. Diabet Med 2005;22: 1295–305.
136. McMahon SK, Airey FL, Marangou DA, et al. Insulin pump therapy in children and adolescents: improvements in key parameters of diabetes management including quality of life. Diabet Med 2005;22:92–6.
137. Houlihan CA, Tsalamandris C, Akdeniz A, et al. Albumin to creatinine ratio: a screening test with limitations. Am J Kidney Dis 2002;39:1183–9.
138. Rocchini AP, Katch V, Anderson J, et al. Blood pressure in obese adolescents: effect of weight loss. Pediatrics 1988;82:16–23.
139. Fischl AFR, Herman WH, Sereika SM, et al. Impact of a preconception counseling program for teens with type 1 diabetes (READY-Girls) on patient-provider interaction, resource utilization, and cost. Diabetes Care 2010;33: 701–5.